Advanc

"Globally recognized as an authority in both the art and science of sales leadership, Helen brings a unique mix of tenacity and humanity to this essential leadership guide, a must-read for every executive committed to exceptional results in our hybrid world. She shares innovative strategies to inspire performance, maximize retention, and build cohesive teams that deliver for shareholders and customers alike. A relentless optimist and gifted storyteller, Helen shows us not only how to survive, but how to THRIVE in one of the most disruptive transformations of our time."

—Robin Fischer Blatt,
Head of Growth, envoyatHome Digital Health

"Helen is the best team-first sales manager I've ever worked for. She consistently worked with me to leverage my strengths, develop my skills, and overcome challenges I faced managing my own team. Helen's focus was always on supporting each team member so we could deliver maximum impact quarter after quarter."

—Leslie Wood,
Senior Director, IoT Sales, Microsoft

"I worked for Helen for two years as a strategic account director, navigating the complexities of one of our most sophisticated and toughest customers. Helen's support, coaching, and ability to overcome internal roadblocks were foundational to my success, allowing us to consistently exceed our ambitious targets. With Helen's guidance and support, I was able to advance my career, get promoted, and move into a sales manager role. Already I am experiencing the subtle power of applying Helen's principles and mentoring to the challenges we all face as sales managers."

—Rahul Maniktala,
Technology Sales Executive, Microsoft

"Helen is truly an example of intelligent leadership. She empowers and enables her employees, always encouraging growth and risk-taking, eliminating roadblocks to success, identifying each person's key strengths and weaknesses, and managing at the individual level to bring out the best in each employee. As a result, the whole of her team is far greater than the sum of its parts, leading to one of the best working environments I've ever experienced."

—Stacey Meston,
Marketing Consultant

"I had the pleasure of reporting to Helen for four years at Sun Microsystems. Helen was a champion for her staff, always willing to try a different approach while continually delivering on our metrics. She showed great appreciation for the work-family life balance and supported her staff to manage that balance. Helen was always willing to do the right thing and ask the hard questions. She is, hands down, the best manager I have had in my career."

—David Charbonneau,
WW Partner Marketing Manager, IBM

"I had the pleasure of working directly with Helen for three years and have known her for over fifteen years. Helen creates high-performing teams that always exceed their goals. Her compassion and loyalty combined with her strong work ethic make Helen an executive you definitely want leading your team."

—Jeff Oberbillig,
Vice President, North America Field Marketing, Red Hat

"Helen is a phenomenal manager. She created a collaborative team environment, irrespective of our geographic location. Her pragmatic guidance provided the support we needed to navigate a complex customer engagement that created a revolutionary market-making service and transformed our business relationship with our customer. I value Helen's personal approach, always being available to provide guidance and simplify complexity."

—Ohad Richberg,
Account Technology Strategist, Microsoft

"I'll never forget my first interaction with Helen. She is helpful, kind, and generous with her time. I admire her leadership and decision-making skills. Her kind words, guidance, and encouragement meant a lot to me. She has been a dedicated mentor and has helped me become a better professional and a better person. I am grateful for every opportunity I get to learn from Helen. She is truly an inspiration!"

—Shivaprasad Mungara,
Technology Strategist, Microsoft

"Helen excels at moving initiatives forward within complex organizational structures. She is creative and is constantly looking for better, more innovative ways to accomplish her objectives and empower her team. Helen is unsurpassed when it comes to managerial courage and forward thinking. She is a strong, authentic leader who any organization would be fortunate to have on board. I would welcome the opportunity to work with her again."

—Julie Lamphiear,

Director, Global Integrated Campaigns—Customer Experience, ServiceNow

"Helen gave me the opportunity to expand my career in high tech and use my executive engagement skills to deliver meaningful business impact. What I most appreciate about Helen is her innate ability to recognize leaders on her team. She gave me the freedom to be the natural leader that I am and excel with great success. Helen is an extraordinary leader and I am grateful for the opportunity that I had to be on her team."

—Peggy Scott,

Presence, Productivity, and Performance Coach

"Helen made a bet on me and gave me the opportunity to pivot my career from the service industry and retail to high tech. She realized my skills were transferrable and could be applied in a tech company. Helen supported my success as I built my skills and network. What I appreciate most about working for Helen is her superpower in creating a team of high performers who make it a joy for all of us to work together."

—Larry Chew,

Senior Briefing Manager, Oracle Corporation

LOVE
YOUR TEAM

A SURVIVAL GUIDE
for Sales Managers in a Hybrid World

HELEN FANUCCI

LIONCREST
PUBLISHING

LOVE YOUR TEAM
A Survival Guide for Sales Managers in a Hybrid World

ISBN 978-1-5445-3401-5 Hardcover
      978-1-5445-3400-8 Paperback
      978-1-5445-3399-5 Ebook
      978-1-5445-3402-2 Audiobook

To my children, Amara and Derek,

You continue to teach me so much about love and life

To my husband, Chris,

You inspire me to be a better version of myself

Contents

PART I
SALES MANAGEMENT, TODAY AND TOMORROW

PART II
THE CONVERSATIONS

PART III
UNIVERSAL CONVERSATIONAL COMPETENCIES

Foreword

When Helen Fanucci first used the phrase "Love Your Team" in a presentation to a room of senior revenue leaders, you could have heard a pin drop—for about five seconds as this radical idea sunk in.

By this point in the conference, everyone had gotten to know Helen as the real deal, a deeply experienced, no-nonsense practitioner of sales management at the highest level, an MIT-trained mechanical engineer who boldly breaks down problems in order to craft practical solutions. The audience was primed for step-by-step advice on how to retain top sales talent in the "new normal" that had arrived sixteen months earlier in March 2020.

The "Great Resignation" was in full swing, and every manager in that room felt queasy when confronting the challenge of keeping their best performers on board and engaged. If you were a sales manager, recruiters were already targeting your sellers with ever-more-attractive offers with powerful incentives to defect, usually to a competitor but also to some hot company in another space. Helen drove that point home, that suddenly the competition for your top talent is not only your traditional competitors but every company in the world. Even I squirmed in my seat a bit—and I knew what was coming, or more correctly, what had already come. An endless global war for top sales talent had broken out, and none of us felt particularly prepared.

Helen had us where she wanted us, paying full attention, hoping for that practical insight that an engineer-turned-sales-manager might drop on us. What we got was utterly unexpected. We got love. But not "love" as an emotion, attitude, or something to make us feel like everything was going to be okay after all. Helen brought love for a different purpose, one that fits her action-oriented way of making progress when facing any challenge. Helen gave us love, and specifically Love Your Team, as an engineering solution to the otherwise intractable problem of surviving this new hybrid world where top talent not only can write their own ticket but decide where they want to cash it in. In other words, a world where the power—all of it—has shifted from us as employers and managers to the individual contributors and team members we rely on to deliver results.

So when Helen dropped the L-bomb, we weren't ready for it. But we listened as she made her case that the new pivot point for sales success had shifted to the humble sales manager for a powerful reason: talented people leave managers, not companies.

Sadly, as Helen shared, most sales managers don't do a fabulous job of being a magnet for top talent. Old-school managers put a rep in a territory and either leave them alone or execute a series of swooping interventions when big deals are on the line. Super-modern managers tinker with sales tools and shiny methodologies in an attempt to get breakthrough performance out of the middle of the pack. And almost every sales manager is distracted by ever-growing data gathering, analysis, and reporting duties and barely has time for occasional one-on-one meetings that almost always focus on some big deal needed to make the quarter. Deal talk, war stories, and strategy suggestions tend to dominate the few sales management conversations that actually do happen.

As we listened to Helen, I believe it dawned on each of us that our traditional approaches put us in peril for one simple reason: they were about what our sales team members could do for us and our company, not what we could do for that team member, both professionally and as a person with a life. Why do I say "peril"? Because in this perpetual war for top talent, our new risk was that some other manager might focus on the desires, needs, and ambitions of our highest performers. That is, we were threatened by anyone recruiting on behalf of a manager who put their team first—who Loved Their Team.

The rest of Helen's talk was both uncomfortable and thrilling. This mechanical engineer was telling us that the physics of business had fundamentally changed, forever, and that we were unlikely to survive unless we changed our ways. That was uncomfortable, especially because she was clearly right. But it was also thrilling because she gave us a way to think about our shared problem differently. She showed us how sales managers can become magnets for top talent. These managers don't just retain top talent but achieve sustained performance that neither old-school approaches nor modern technology and methodologies can deliver. We just needed to Love Our Teams.

But a talk at a conference can only teach us so much. Where was the program we could follow to transition to this powerful way of managing? The answer is here in your hands. Encouraged by that audience's response to the Love Your Team concept, followed by many hours of conversation and exploration, Helen took on the massive task of writing this book. She means the title to be taken literally—especially the part about it being a "Survival Guide for Sales Managers in a Hybrid World." The world is not going back to the good old days when our employees had lots of community and family anchors that also bound them to the office and therefore their job. The hybrid world of work from anywhere is here to stay, and it's time for us to practically adapt, step by step, conversation by conversation to this new reality.

I think this book should be read once through in order to get what that audience in 2021 got: that the Love Your Team approach makes sense and is worth the effort to adopt. But much more importantly, this book is a survival guide, providing you with a practical framework and detailed instructions for how to hold all of the many types of conversations you must master to make Love Your Team work in the rough-and-tumble world of complex, big-ticket sales. Some of these conversations may be unfamiliar, and others will be uncomfortable. But like the many tools on a good survival knife, each and every one has its time and place. You will find yourself reaching for this book repeatedly to get a quick reminder of how to choose the right conversation, plan, and prepare to conduct it and assess that conversation's impact. And you will not just survive; you will enjoy and thrive along your journey in the most pivotal role in modern business: sales manager.

—Chris Beall
CEO, ConnectAndSell

Foreword

I f there's one thing a Silicon Valley tech career has taught me, it's that the latest and greatest sales management technique has the shelf life of a banana.

As soon as an organization is trained, certified, and onboarded to the revolutionary new approach that has the final word on breakthrough performance, Executive Team 2.0 (or 3.0 or 4.0) escorts the next fleece-vest-clad band of management consultants into the techy-posh headquarters building to start the process all over again. And again.

It may sound like I think this is a cosmic waste of time and resources, but on the contrary, constant reinvention is the secret to keeping a sales organization humming at peak performance.

Despite a clever title paying homage to the Wharton (or Stanford or, in Helen's case, MIT) genius who pioneered it, there's one thing that every sales management approach has in common, and when well executed, the result is magic. Helen has captured this magic in her deceptively simple book. I say deceptively simple because her writing is easily digestible and immediately applicable, but her approach is based on sophisticated behavioral science and proven technique.

The three Es—Empathy, Execution discipline, and Emotional intelligence—are the foundation of what Helen teaches when she shows us how to love our teams. From the anxious control freak micromanager to the one who espouses "I believe in empowerment" as a transparent excuse to avoid difficult conversations, Helen creates a safe place to learn—or in my case, to revisit—the fundamental conversations that turn geographically dispersed individuals into a productive, resilient sales engine.

Helen and I learned how to lead from the three Es when we worked together at Sun Microsystems. That extraordinary experience carried us through fruitful careers in high-performance sales organizations. Although we went in different directions after Sun, each of us continued to benefit from the gift of exceptional role models, training from the best subject matter experts in the business, and the privilege of working with incredible salespeople who prove that sales isn't just a job; it's a profession. (We also worked for duds, characters, and individuals of questionable intent, but those are stories for the next book!)

A hybrid or remote work environment has long been part of the culture and norm for many companies. But for sales managers newly adapting to pandemic-driven distributed teams, Helen gives step-by-step instructions on how to build a cadence of individual and group engagement to show your team the love they need to deliver the goods. It's the love that fosters employee retention, increases sales productivity, helps people stuck in the wrong job gracefully (and gratefully) move on, and produces results that exceed expectations not in spite of remote work but because of it.

I can't predict whether remote/hybrid work will outlive a banana, but I can say with confidence that the three Es—and Helen's techniques for putting them to work—will endure.

The bottom line is that professionals deserve a great manager, and the first step to becoming one is to take Helen's lead and love our teams.

—**Robin Fischer Blatt**
Head of Growth, envoyatHome Digital Health
Leader, Coach, Mentor, Board Member

Introduction

THE GREAT POWER SHIFT—TOP TALENT RULES!

When I first became a manager, I thought I needed to tell my team how to do their job. Fortunately, I quickly learned to focus instead on the outcome expected and treat my sellers with respect and trust, letting them deliver superior results in ways that consistently surpassed anything I could imagine. Even more importantly, my top talent would stay on board, meeting those outcomes while helping each other out, even though they were almost always being recruited by competitors.

This experience formed the basis of my management approach and the way I build high-performing teams while strengthening team culture, although we did not use the word *culture* much in those days. I've learned a few more things since and realized that to build a high-performing team and retain talent, it is critical to promptly address underperforming team members. I've expanded my thinking on what culture is and how to create and maintain a positive one even when my employer's culture had room for improvement.

But this level of performance and team stability required more than just focusing on results and staying out of their way. It took management work—lots of it. Almost all of that work was in the form of conversations between sellers on my team and me, their manager. To make sure my teams were successful, I learned that I needed to prioritize having the right conversations at the right times with each of my sellers. There were always demands to do other things—planning, reporting, training, and more—but having effective conversations with my sellers was the bedrock of their performance and my success. Those conversations with my team needed to come first, ahead of those traditional activities that seem to fill every sales manager's calendar.

Of course, every sales manager knows the importance of conversations with sellers to set objectives. Without these conversations, your team would not be accountable for anything, and results will be a matter of chance.

But there's another kind of conversation that gets less attention from traditional sales managers: conversations with the express purpose of helping sellers as needed by them, on their terms. These are the conversations that make or break your team, both in terms of consistently producing results and, as importantly, inspiring your sellers to want to stay on *your* team, especially in our new "hybrid world" where your top talent can walk out the door without taking a single step.

Over time, I recognized that these conversations had grown into a system I could consistently use to help my sellers be successful and find satisfaction in their jobs while proudly contributing to winning together, achieving their professional and earnings goals, and staying and growing to do it all again—only better.

At the core of this system of conversations is a simple principle: Love Your Team. As a sales manager, your team needs more than direction and correction. They need your help along the way. Love Your Team? Whoa, what's that? This does not sound like a business book, but more of a feel-good, do-good book. Yes, I get it. It is, however, profoundly pragmatic, reliably delivering exceptional, sustainable business results.

THE HYBRID WORLD OF TODAY AND TOMORROW

In July 2021, I was giving a keynote at a conference for sales leaders in Dallas, Texas. I was excited. This was my first time traveling and being around fellow professionals since the pandemic started. My topic was "Sales Leadership in a Hybrid World." It was already evident we were facing a severe talent shortage with 4.5 million people quitting their jobs every month. When I got to the part of the presentation on retaining talent, I struggled to find the right words to clearly express what I believed sales managers must do to retain their top performers. This is what I ended up putting on my PowerPoint slide: "Love Your Team." I was nervous. How would the audience react? It's weird to use the term *love* in a business context, right? I went with it anyway and talked about what it means to Love Your Team. The audience responded instantly. I got such great feedback that it gave me the confidence to use it as the title for this book. I even launched my own podcast in January 2022 called, you guessed it, *Love Your Team*, exploring strategies for retaining talent and building high-performing sales teams with other successful sales managers.

At the core of the Love Your Team system is my purpose as a manager: set objectives and support my team along the way as needed. The first should be familiar to traditional sales managers. The second is not.

But this second element actually makes or breaks your team. To effectively support your team in your capacity as manager, you have to Love Your Team. It's the only way to keep your people and deliver top results. It's how you survive and thrive as a sales manager in the new world of hybrid work.

Hybrid work is defined as a flexible configuration of how and where we work: some of us at the office, some remote, and some splitting their time between the two. More and more employees also demand flexibility of not just where but when they work. Work has become more asynchronous and the collaboration tools of today make this a real option. Traditional management, accustomed to a factory-style bullpen floor filled with homogenous workers, struggles to adapt. If you fail to adapt, you can quickly find yourself with an exodus of top sellers, managing trickle-up job dissatisfaction, missing sales quotas, and facing the very real threat of being replaced.

Of course, the world has been changing for decades. But the COVID-19 pandemic hammered the last nail in the coffin of the good ol' days of good ol' boy sales management. Traditional hands-off sales management no longer works in today's hybrid world of remote work, with top talent demanding a job that works for them.

We all know we must adapt. But what should we focus on amid all the noise and uncertainty that fills our lives as sales managers? The answer is "retention." Retention is key. If a company can't retain its talent, it risks going out of business. If you as manager can't retain the talent on your team, you risk your career. Talent is the key to competitiveness and innovation. It's the key to revenue and growth.

Without motivated, committed talent, you and your company are in peril.

In the innovation economy, sales talent is the link to growth and company valuation. This puts sales managers at the unrecognized pivot point to multiply team success and retain top talent. Without effective sales management capable of attracting and retaining talent by adapting to changing requirements and the expectations of top sellers, every company is at risk of becoming an Innovation Age dinosaur, left behind while others dominate fast-developing markets.

We, as sales managers, can't just hire and fire our way out of performance problems anymore. Hiring replacements is stunningly expensive—often costing as much as a seller's entire quota—and all you get is another shot at retaining a top performer. The question is: how are you going to attract, grow, and retain top talent in a world where anybody can work from anywhere and every company, whether a business competitor or not, is now your real competitor in the never-ending war for talent?

The short answer: support your people.

From my decades of managerial experience and observations of what works, I provide here practical and actionable conversational strategies every sales manager can use to effectively support their sellers. The key is to treat your team members as whole people with lives and ambitions worthy of your attention while simultaneously supporting their job performance and professional development.

In this book, I share with you how to Love Your Team to get top results.

It all starts with conversations. After all, how do you know the support your team needs if you don't ask, listen, and understand? This book will show you how to choose and execute the exact conversations each seller needs in every management situation you must address to free them to execute successfully while making them want to stay on board with you.

But before we get to when and how to hold these conversations, I want to provide some background on why they are so necessary.

THE COST OF ATTRITION

Your top seller with a $1 million quota resigns on day one of the new fiscal year. The likely cost starts with $750,000 of lost quota attainment. But this is understated as you not only lose the value of the lost revenue while you hire and ramp a replacement, but you also lose the value of the future revenue streams and renewals from those customers you failed to capture while you were short a top seller. Additionally, top sellers who leave often take other good sellers with them. When one seller leaves, it is not uncommon to see others go.

- Three months to hire a replacement — $250,000 in lost revenue attainment

- Six months for seller to be productive — $500,000 in lost revenue attainment

And after all that, maybe your replacement seller works out. Too often they don't. If they don't, you get to start all over again, starting in an even deeper hole than you were in with the first departure.

WOULD YOU WORK FOR YOU?

We often think of companies like Big Brother, watching and controlling our actions to meet their goals. In truth, a company is a collection of people working together toward a common goal—and as a manager you are the pivot point for your team achieving their goals. If you put quota attainment ahead of your people, you will fail to provide them with a supportive culture, you will have no real team, and they will have little ability to deliver predictably consistent results. For a team member to believe their career and life are best served by working for you as their manager, you must understand each of their motivations and goals and then support them in attaining the life and career they desire.

When Satya Nadella took over as Microsoft's CEO in 2014, he made culture a top priority. Microsoft has since evolved to be people focused. In 2021, during an interview with a senior editor at *Harvard Business Review*, Satya proposed a thought experiment: instead of thinking about how each employee works for the company, think about how the company works for each employee.[1]

This is what sales leaders need to think about as well. How will each of our employees evaluate us, their sales manager, when they reflect on whether or not their job is working for them?

Here's my thought experiment for you: would you work for you?

---

[1] "Microsoft's Satya Nadella on Flexible Work, the Metaverse, and the Power of Empathy," interview by Adi Ignatius, *Harvard Business Review*, October 28, 2021, https://hbr.org/2021/10/microsofts-satya-nadella-on-flexible-work-the -metaverse-and-the-power-of-empathy.

Gallup tells us that 70 percent of an employee's experience is based on their interactions with their manager. Managers are vital to an employee's feeling of well-being and job satisfaction. They are the gatekeepers to resources and promotion. They are often both judge and executioner. And they can either be a team member's biggest help or hindrance to getting their job done.

It's a new orientation, especially for those companies lagging behind the employee development curve. The data clearly says employees now want more from their company in terms of aligned values and work environment—money is no longer enough. They also want more from their manager in terms of work flexibility, empathy, understanding, and accommodation of their work situation and more.

While the pandemic brought these changing requirements into sharp view, for many they have always been there, especially for women with children navigating the world of work. In the late 1990s, when my children were three and six years old, I got divorced and ended up with sole custody and sole financial responsibility for my children. I was overwhelmed. Some days I was not sure I could keep my head above water at work while managing the demands of my daily life; getting my kids up in the morning, to school or childcare, commuting for an hour to work, working, commuting another hour back to pick them up by 6:00 p.m., feed them dinner, complete homework, get them ready for bed, respond to work emails, go to bed. Repeat. I was fortunate to find high school or college-age girls with a car who could pick up my kids in the late afternoon and feed them dinner. When my kids were sick, I was fortunate enough to be able to either bring them into the office, as we all had private offices back then, or work from home. That eased the situation for me. This flexibility made my life work. I'm eternally grateful for the managers I had during those times who allowed me to shift where and when I worked when the demands of being a mother and primary caregiver took precedence. Their willingness to embrace "hybrid work" more than twenty years before the term was invented was a lifesaver and a lesson for me, both personally and professionally.

In March 2020, the pandemic drove this point home for both employers and employees. Businesses and employees suddenly needed to adapt or fail.

In March 2020, companies were forced to empty their offices of everyone who could work from home. In one fell swoop, this wholesale shift accelerated the trend of moving to flexible working conditions, embracing practices the tech sector had been honing for decades. The shift happened suddenly, across industries and jobs that no one thought could be done from home. Satya Nadella observed that the world experienced two years of transformation in two months.

In the new hybrid world forced upon all industries by the pandemic, workers across the board suddenly got to experience the benefits and challenges of this new flexibility. While there seemed no end to challenges in terms of dealing with kids being schooled at home, reconfiguring living spaces into work spaces, and finding a quiet moment to preserve their sanity, workers also got an unexpected bonus: flexibility. Whether it was what they wore, or didn't wear, on the job; when they worked and when they took some time off to tend to personal or family matters; or whether they even continued to live within commuting distance of their office was entirely their call. Workers started to think differently about their relationship to their jobs. They adapted and their priorities shifted permanently.

For management, adaptation seemed to come more slowly and often reluctantly. For example, I know of a large company whose CEO dictated in 2021 that everyone return to the office. Every day, he counted the cars in the parking lot to see how many employees came into the office. The result? Employees resigned in droves, and top talent was the first out the door.

Even in manufacturing industries, the employee who dedicated himself to the company for the entirety of his career has become a thing of the past. I have an acquaintance in Arizona who worked for Boeing for decades. In 2021, he told me he'd quit if they required him to go back to the office in Seattle. They did. He left.

Many workers now also want to work for a purpose-driven organization that shares their values, and these values are not limited to human rights, immigration law, sustainable practices, or social justice. Workers' personal values are rooted in their families and communities and can be supported by working conditions that make participation in family and community possible. They have ambitions and career goals. They have lives. To be competitive in a tight job market, companies need to show, first and foremost, that they are dedicated to their employees and what they care about.

In what some call the Great Resignation or Great Reshuffle of 2021, 60 percent of employees reported they considered leaving their company and their job to explore new opportunities. That's partly why there's a talent shortage. Jobs are going unfilled as people leave for organizations, roles, and work situations they believe might serve them better. And when top talent leaves a company whose culture and management style is unattractive, good luck backfilling those roles.

The pandemic disrupted women's career and work life disproportionately compared to men's. Women are still the primary childcare and elderly caregivers in our society. They resigned in droves to take care of family needs. Most have not returned to a permanent job and perhaps they never will. They are redesigning their lives and work, starting their own companies or taking gig-economy roles to work on their own terms rather than go back to work for "the man" who does not support their goals and life situation.

As I write this in May 2022, there is a lot of talk about an upcoming recession. Will the talent shortage last? I'm already seeing companies lay off workers and freeze hiring, especially in the tech sector. While the numbers might someday show the talent shortage easing up, there will always be a need for top sales talent. Top talent is always scarce and top performers can always write their own ticket in any job market. Top talent is the best investment a company can make with outsized returns. And, from now on, that investment must be made in not just dollars but in flexibility, support, and caring.

In today's world, talent is not centralized. Not long ago, companies picked headquarters colocated near the talent pools they needed, pools created by ivy-covered universities and the collection of glass-and-steel headquarters of similar companies. Upon getting a job, employees would usually relocate to within commuting distance of the company headquarters. Companies could pick and choose among the concentrated talent that had moved to be close to all those potential employers. But that's all gone now. The free ride companies enjoyed by being colocated near talent pools is over. Because people can work from anywhere, the talent is spread everywhere—and companies now must compete not just within their industry and geography but across all industries and across the entire globe.

You might be saying, "Wait a minute; I need to hire sellers who live close to the customer." But where is the customer now? Are executive decision makers in their office every day, or have they moved to an inviting location of their choice? Sure, in-person meetings are still important, but in the hybrid world they more likely will happen infrequently and be organized well in advance. Customer executives and sellers will routinely fly to a central location for an executive briefing, or maybe meet in person in conjunction with an industry conference.

Pandemic or post-pandemic, hybrid work is here to stay. Today's managers must facilitate work across regions, often across countries, coordinating time zones and unending combinations of remote and in-person communication among their teams, customers, and executives. Companies are scrambling to develop their hybrid policies, work strategies, infrastructure, and expectations. It's a moving target that will keep moving for the foreseeable future, but one thing won't move: top talent will demand flexibility, and they will get it.

MANAGERS HOLD THE KEY TO RETENTION

While you and I as managers may not have the ability to set the tone for the whole company, we always have the opportunity to set a tone for our team that makes our talent want to stay. Our sellers are listening to us. If we don't communicate clearly so they understand and become invested in the bigger picture, they will start listening to someone who does. Ultimately, they will decide to stay or leave based on how our management style works for them. They can always find a different employer. It's up to us as managers to make our team and their job work for them so they choose to continue to work with us. Your number one seller just became your most important customer.

In the global innovation economy, top talent is always in hot demand. The result is a massive shift of power to employees. Employees have options, and those options drive up their expectations, especially for flexibility. They will go where their priorities—career, community, family—are best served. It's the talent that now creates competitive advantage, especially in the sphere of innovation. At first, it might feel like a few people are leaving a company in ones and twos; but over time, it's death by a thousand cuts, with no way to stop the bleeding.

During the 2021 and 2022 COVID variant surges, even the mighty Amazon vacillated, first mandating all employees be in the office, then only requiring in-office work a few days a week. Eventually they gave up the corporate one-size-fits-all approach and handed power over to the team leaders—the managers—who each determined a policy that would work locally for their team. This is a sign of the times. Managers are the pivot point between teams and company executives. If that pivot fails or is too rigid, productivity plummets and employees leave.

To retain talent that demands flexibility, a company and its managers also have to become flexible. In Amazon's case, they are empowering the managers who are closest to the action to determine how that team gets their best work done. Sales managers must employ the same trust-building and empathy with their team members as they do with their customers and examine what employees want and need and adjust accordingly. The most effective managers adjust to their team, not the other way around.

The tech sector is leading in the race to be more adaptable to hybrid work because, after all, they invented the tools for it. My employer, Microsoft, is the original work-from-home company, made possible by Bill Gates's vision of a computer in every home. By necessity, more traditional practices in more traditional industries will shift over time, with many already surprising themselves by discovering that hybrid work generates higher productivity and employee engagement than their traditional model.

The company with the car-counting CEO had a hard time attracting people to fill their vacancies. Their location was not ideal for many. The company had to look elsewhere for talent. It showed the cracks in the hard-nosed approach of requiring people to come to the office. Finally the Delta variant hit and the company sent everybody home again, providing another opportunity to rethink their approach to employees and decide what was most important to their company's health. They struggle to adapt, but ultimately they have no choice.

We've exited the Industrial Age of factory-style knowledge work, and COVID showed companies, in case there was any doubt, that every company needs to be a tech company to survive. They need to become agile and adopt a digital-first strategy in order to compete: flexibility, hybrid work, and the tools and technology that engage and enable global collaborative work have become necessities.

But while other aspects of company work have been leaping forward, sales managers—those all-important pivot points between executives and employees—have lagged woefully behind.

RISKY BUSINESS

Buyer expectations, much like those of workers, are changing too. Eighty percent of buyers want to buy from organizations whose teams are diverse, but 80.2 percent of Americans in sales-related occupations are not diverse. These numbers don't match. This reflects a broader generational shift, as younger generations rise into professional ranks and companies cater to global audiences, diverse sales forces are needed to provide more trust and value to buyers.

In the innovation economy, a seller is not just moving inventory churned out by a factory; they're selling technology and related services—new ways of getting complex jobs done more efficiently and effectively. There are few standards or specifications. The premium is on innovating new solutions that must somehow be integrated into existing systems, infrastructure, data, and policies.

Business buyers have always been cautious, but now every purchase decision is fraught with even more risk when a new solution doesn't pan out. Whether it's because the technology is complicated, takes extensive training, is technically incompatible, or takes too long to implement, every purchase seems to touch every part of the buyer's organization. This puts a premium on speed for sellers. Often, it's the seller that can get to the buyer fastest who wins, locking out competing products, because what buyer wants to change to a different platform once the current one is embedded in the organization?

All this pressure on buyers means that sellers are more critical than ever to the success of every company in the innovation economy. Buyers don't want to risk their own careers by making a poor decision. Sales is now the choke point for monetizing innovations in the market. Sellers need to sell risk reduction along with the solution. Sellers must establish trust and build strong relationships in order to be accepted by buyers. This takes skill, finesse, and the ability to be accepted as a true expert, bringing the right resources to bear to not only sell the solution but ensure it actually delivers the value the buyer expects. Those skills don't appear overnight. Sellers need time and learning resources to help them grow and keep up with the pace of innovation. A seller who is good enough today becomes irrelevant tomorrow unless they find a way to keep up with relentless change.

As sales managers, we can foster this growth. We can lead the way, provide the model, set the tone, coach, and make sure our sellers have the time and resources to stay sharp. We are the catalysts for productivity and effectiveness today and skills and knowledge improvement for tomorrow.

If the world is changing rapidly, then how we sell—and how we manage this selling—needs to change with it. As sales managers in the innovation economy, we must adapt to the realities of hybrid work to effectively hire, develop, and retain team members who also possess the ability to navigate and adapt to ever-increasing complexity.

WILL SEARCH REPLACE SELLERS?

You've probably seen recent discussions that claim search engines will eventually replace the role of sellers and sales managers, even in enterprise sales. I disagree.

Enterprise sales are large and complex. Enterprises are elaborate entities, with committees and consensus in place of autonomous decision makers. Compounding this complexity, especially if you work for an enterprise that sells to other enterprises, is your own organization's many stakeholders and the layers of approval each deal has to navigate. For example, as an enterprise seller, no matter what my title is or how much dealmaking authority I might appear to have, I cannot come up with a deal discount by myself. I must go to the deal desk and make my case—and that's after I have gotten consensus on my team that a discount is the right move. Complex and shifting layers of influence and approval ultimately determine what is offered, how a deal is structured, and what resources will be brought to bear. Hundreds of conversations end up shaping each deal, whether it gets done or falls through.

And not one of these conversations can be effectively held by a machine or search engine that doesn't understand the first thing about the evolving relationships, motivations, situations, desires, and fears of this ever-shifting cast of characters that make up both sides of every deal.

In other words, if you work as a sales manager in this hybrid world, you better be a real human being who gets your fellow human beings—your sellers. Mastering the conversations presented in this book will help you put your humanity in service to your team, no matter what the future brings.

THE PROOF IS IN THE DATA

I've been managing remote employees for over twenty-five years. Some of the largest teams I have managed were when I worked for Sun Microsystems. My team members worked from home across the US and Europe as well as in the office in our headquarters location in Silicon Valley. I refined my style and approach to managing teams through observing what worked and what didn't. I learned that when I empowered my team and stayed out of their way, the top performers delivered. I learned how to identify underperforming employees and what conversations and actions to take to address performance issues. I learned that providing flexibility where and when possible was not only a good idea but gained me the trust and loyalty of my team. I learned that in order to be a great manager that people wanted to work for, I needed to understand my team members, their lives, their needs, and their ambitions and support them where and how I could. Sometimes I managed teams of sellers.

Other times I managed marketing teams. I've managed technical teams and sales operations teams. While this book focuses on sales management and retaining top-talent sellers, the ideas and underlying approach I've come to call Love Your Team work across virtually all management roles because people are people no matter what job they are doing and, by and large, they have common needs, goals, and desires.

The conversations and data on which this book is based come from these decades of experience. At one point, I became curious about my own work and effectiveness. I started noting the types of conversations I was having with my team and the broader internal team to support the outcomes and goals expected of me and my team. I logged how often I had each type of conversation. I know now that four types of conversations comprise 63 percent of my conversational time with my team. These detailed insights into what effective sales managers actually do on the ground, using myself as a case study, underpin the guidance and how-tos given in this survival guide.

This book also grew out of my desire to help others and share my experience. I have mentored many other sales managers. I see how some sales leaders hurt their own effectiveness by focusing on quota attainment and ignoring the people side of the business. My goal is to share what I've learned with you and make it actionable so that you can immediately put it into practice. My unique boots-on-the-ground point of view on managing teams resonates with those who want to know how to love their team better. I'm now a frequent speaker at sales leadership conferences and a guest on podcasts, and I've started my own podcast called *Love Your Team* to share strategies to help sales managers retain their top talent and build high-performing teams.

SALES MANAGEMENT IS MORE THAN CLOSING A DEAL

Many sales management books outline best practices for sellers and how to be a great sales manager. These books typically cover topics such as effective cold-calling, building pipeline, relationships, or consultative selling skills. Sometimes they even cover techniques for closing a sale.

However, there is very little information out there on how to effectively manage and develop a team of sellers. This book is a how-to survival guide for enterprise sales managers that shares the skills and strategies for retaining top-talent sellers. It outlines the conversations that are necessary for effective sales leadership and building high-performing sales teams in business-to-business enterprise sales companies. This is not self-help. If you're reading this book, you most likely recognize the need to do something differently and you just need the basic vocabulary, theory, and actions to do it.

This book is divided into three parts. The first part gives context and the foundational principles for holding the conversations central to the Love Your Team approach to sales management.

The second part is a step-by-step survival guide, a how-to of the core conversations I conduct with my team when I take this approach. For each conversation, I outline:

- Its purpose
- Intended outcomes
- How to recognize the need for the conversation
- How to conduct it
- Assessing if it worked
- Considerations

The third part of the book briefs you on the skills and culture you will need to carry out these conversations to full effect.

This book is intended to be a survival guide, a how-to book for having effective conversations with your team that drive business results and sales performance. It offers guidance and support as you encounter specific conversational opportunities that will increase your team's success. The conversations are arranged in a suggested reading order that goes from the first time you meet your team through performance expectations and internal alignment. By their nature, the conversations that come later in the book may not make sense to a given seller on your team if you haven't had the foundational conversations that appear in the earlier chapters.

For instance, if you as a manager haven't laid out clear performance expectations in conversations with your team, then a conversation about underperformance with a team member will be confusing at best. They have to know what to do and to what standard before you can talk to them about results that may or may not meet those standards.

But I acknowledge everyone comes to this information from their own experiences and priorities, so each conversational chapter in Part II is written to stand alone and be read out of sequence. In short, you'll get some big-picture benefits from reading the book in its present order, but the book is designed so each conversation chapter can stand alone to help you and your team each day.

AT THE END OF THE DAY

The key to avoiding extinction is adaptation. And sales managers are the missing link to optimizing this adaptation to maximize fitness in the new hybrid world.

You, as a sales manager, are in an excellent position to adopt strategies and practices that will help you and your team thrive in this new sales paradigm.

To effectively employ these strategies, it's important to clearly define your role and responsibilities as a Love Your Team sales manager and to recognize that the old sales management style is still entrenched in many sales forces. You may even have to make the pitch to other decision makers in your company to let you give these strategies a go, and you might benefit from having some history as a foundation for advocating change.

So, what's different about the sales world today that makes the case for changing your approach to sales management?

PART I

SALES MANAGEMENT, TODAY AND TOMORROW

CHAPTER 1

From Myth to Management

Have you looked at job postings for seeking sellers lately? The job requirements are vast. The expectations are high across so many dimensions. Who is that mythical seller anyway and how do you find them? I once heard a sales manager say he only hired closers: top sellers who could do it all and most importantly close deals. He determined this by having potential hires go through a character profiling test run by a third party. If the seller checked all the boxes, they, obviously, had no flaws and would get hired. They would far exceed their quota, and everyone would live happily ever after. Right?

The idea of an unflawed person is, of course, absurd. It implies the world, and people, are unchanging, that what worked in the past will always work in the future. There's a deep-seated belief in traditional sales management that sales skills are fixed and that what worked in the past still works today and will still work in the future. It's a fantasy. A fairy tale. A myth.

Traditionally, it was thought that a sales manager need only put an ad in the newspaper (yes, I'm referring to traditional print media) with the criterion "only closers need apply," which then garnered résumés from hundreds of top sellers who could, when hired, be assigned a territory, left alone, and magically meet revenue targets with nothing but a clap on the back. The sales manager's only responsibilities were to hire talent with the chops to make their quotas and fire them if they failed. Sellers were put in a sales territory with some knowledge of the product but minimal to no training or coaching on how to sell it to customers. Since they were unflawed, the sellers, of course, needed no development. And since skills were fixed, if the seller didn't have them, well, they'd never learn.

There are many downsides to this traditional approach, one of which is that it often deters nontraditional candidates from applying for a job. It makes it more expensive to find good candidates and disenfranchises the current team in place when they read it (and they will) if they believe they're not good enough for you OR you're not working hard enough on their behalf to get more help on the team.

Even many executives believe that the role of a sales manager is to hire sellers, give them a territory, and hope they work out. If they don't, fire them. Nothing ventured, nothing gained. The sales manager finds another seller and repeats the process. Unfortunately, hope is not a strategy for success. As we've seen, enterprise sales managers must have an updated *and updating* skillset. Actually managing and supporting the success of sellers is critical, especially in a world where talent is scarce. Sellers today expect their managers to understand them and know them, have empathy, and provide coaching and guidance when needed. They expect sales managers to remove roadblocks and sales friction and empower their success.

Companies demand that sales managers have the skills necessary to build a high-performing team, deliver on revenue and quota expectations, and create a sustainable and predictable sales model. However, as is often the case, while companies' expectations are high, their focus on developing sales managers to have the right skills is low to nonexistent. It is rare indeed to find a company that focuses on empathetic leadership skills, building trust and tapping into your team's motivations as an approach to creating high-performance teams. Sales managers are then left to figure out their own skill development by reading books or more typically listening to audiobooks, podcasts, or getting tips from others.

Managers who are promoted from within the work group have an extra responsibility to build trust, especially if multiple team members were applicants. This adds more complexity to the manager onboarding and trust dynamic. New managers are tempted to micromanage, trying to make an impact all at once. This can also be exacerbated if some team members are colocated with the new manager and others are remote, feeling alienated as outsiders.

Because of their antiquated attitude, traditional sales managers are not skilled coaches. They cannot teach their sellers how to be effective in the specific context of this company that has this product for these customers. "Coaching," for traditional managers, consists of telling war stories about their past selling exploits: what they did to move a sale forward or get a bigger deal. If a seller doesn't work out, they get put on a performance improvement plan, which is code for the company's exit lane. There is no coaching or training included in that PIP. Just telling someone to improve doesn't work;

you have to show the team member how to improve, coaching and checking in throughout that development. You have to provide opportunities for the team member to get the missing skills. And it's becoming less clear what skillsets lead to the best performance in the future, so ongoing development is key.

Sales have changed, sellers have changed, and managers need to catch up and ground themselves in the reality of management, rather than the myth.

A BRIEF HISTORY OF SALES MANAGEMENT

Then, the Tradition

The original purpose of sales was to dispense physical inventory and products. The front office was the actual front of the factory that made those products. Products were physical, mechanical, consistent, external.

Sellers were seen the same way. I've heard managers describe their employees as coin-operated machines. In fact, some company leaders still wonder why sales can't be managed with the predictability of their factory. If only we could have a predictable sales process and training, the sellers would crank out closed deals like the factory workers crank out widgets. Sellers who do what they're told, punch a time clock, and work their shift would provide predictable results. Sellers were expected to fit their lives into their work. Be available at all hours to the sales manager's beck and call. Always prioritize critical work activities over personal desires like vacation or family leave.

Right up to the start of COVID, it was customary for sellers to work in a bullpen environment. This tradition has gone on as long as I've been selling. This image of sellers on the phones with the manager overseeing the action is not so far removed from old Industrial Age photos of garment factory workers sitting in one room sewing.

Over time, sellers who regularly used to meet with customers at their office stopped coming into the office on a regular basis. They would come into the office and sit in the bullpen when they needed to focus on building pipeline, cold-calling and creating new opportunities. A typical sales floor was abuzz with sellers talking. There were, and still are, blitz days where sellers are expected to devote their time cold-calling to generate new pipelines. Now the blitz days are done remotely. Before COVID, they were done on a sales floor with the sales managers walking around, listening to conversations, coaching, and keeping score on who was generating the most new opportunities or the biggest pipeline during the blitz. Even though we talk about teams as groups of people working toward one goal, in reality, it's more a collection of individuals competing against each other. And traditional sales managers foster this competition. But when you are competitive you don't want to share resources and knowledge, because then the other guy might beat you. So opportunities for learning and growth and connection and collegiality are missed. Productivity suffers. When productivity suffers, the company suffers.

I know traditional sales managers who miss this buzz and action. They loved to ring the bell signifying a deal closed or a big opportunity being created during a blitz. This rah-rah type of sales management misses the point. Today's top sellers are not laborers. They know that their value is more than a number and they can work wherever they choose. They have honed their craft and continue to learn. They care much more about taking care of their career and family than today's deal.

Now, the Innovation

There is less predictability in sales now compared to the past when products were easy to understand and widgets came off the assembly line without much variation. In today's innovation economy, traditional manufacturers are shifting from being product companies to services companies. As an example, Honeywell, the century-old industrial company, is reinventing itself to be an industrial software company and utilizes data to provide value-added services to the products it builds and sells. This is happening in every company on the planet today. Innovate, use data and services to differentiate offerings or perish.

Instead of sellers dispensing physical inventory as was their job in the past, they must now sell intangible and often complex solutions that depend on customers being able to use them, integrate them, and derive value from them based on how they are implemented in the customer's environment. Sellers must be able to build trust and help the customer through their buying journey, which includes upwards of ten decision makers for an average enterprise sale. There are new stakeholders at the customer's table who have veto power. These are legal, compliance, human resources, line of business executives, sustainability officers, privacy, security, information technology, CTO, etc. It is a dizzying array of executive stakeholders, all with a different agenda and decision criteria. The seller must be able to overcome any perceived risk the buyers may have. In many cases, these buyers are betting their careers and the reputation of their companies on their buying decision.

We see this in the consumer market as well. A Tesla is a computer on wheels. Your average mechanic can't touch it with a ten-foot pole. Tesla is not just selling a car. They are selling value-added services, such as convenient charging stations and predictive maintenance along with use of data and AI to make the car safer to drive. With Tesla, buyers are buying the brand, fun of driving, and the extras, which appeal to our inner geek as much as the physical car.

Transactional selling is dead. There is no wham, bam, thank you ma'am, no bell-ringing, no "rah-rah!" yelling from the sales manager. It is no longer viable for a seller to transact and walk away. Closing a sale signifies the beginning of a long journey with the customer. They are placing trust in your ability to deliver. Customers expect the seller and the company the seller works for to help them use what they bought. The buyer and their company are making a bet-your-business decision and expect a trust-based enduring relationship. Many, if not most, organizations now have a customer success function whose role is to help customers get value from what they bought. Notice I did not say activate or use what they bought. That is a transactional mindset as well. Use does not equal value. Customers expect to get value and value as defined by them. This is much different from sales and services of the past. This is the new frontier of selling, ensuring that what you sell is actually delivering the value the customer expects.

Sales management is people management, since it's people making those sales decisions on both sides of the table (or computer screen). I've heard traditional sales managers say, "It's just about delivering the results; give those coin-operated sellers a quota and they'll go after it. Great sellers are born, not developed; they don't need anything but a direction." How antiquated do you have to be to find coin-operated anything now? Even the metaphor is obsolete, a remnant of a coin-operated time when machines were much simpler and it was expected employees would perform for a simple transaction: I pay, you deliver. That time is over.

Like cars and computers, people are much more complicated today, especially with COVID at their backs showing them their own vulnerabilities and reminding everyone they are, in fact, mortal. The old boys' club kind of transactional, hands-off management is not winning in the hybrid world. Management now requires time, attention, and love. It requires working with and for people.

If you are not genuinely invested in your team, if you don't care about them, if you don't love them, don't be their manager. Find another job.

Effective sales management requires being focused on your team, as individuals and as a collective whole. The connection and trust you build one person at a time sets the tone for the team and provides the building blocks for a strong and positive culture. Be invested in each person and the team as a whole. Have a desire for everyone to succeed. Think, "It's a journey, and we all want to arrive at the end" versus, "It's a sport, and only the best person wins." The investment in each person happens in the conversations, interactions, and subsequent actions you take to support their success. It is through these conversations that you learn about them as a person, what they care about, and where they need help and support to be successful. It's a different managerial approach, a Love Your Team approach, and is the key to survival for sales managers in today's world.

BEST PRACTICES FOR ENTERPRISE SALES MANAGERS

As mentioned in the Introduction, one of the biggest myths in sales management is that managers know best and need to tell their team what to do. However, I've found it's much more effective and powerful to unleash my talented team's creativity.

To do this as an enterprise sales manager, you need some basic skills:

- Have trust and relationship-building skills.
- Set measurable outcome-based expectations.
- Create an operational cadence to assess whether or not your team is on track.
- Provide opportunities for coaching and support when team members need it.
- Understand the needs of your team members and accommodate where possible.

- Have a team communication strategy to ensure everyone keeps informed and is aware when something changes as it invariably will.
- Ensure you can accommodate in-person and remote communication and follow inclusive practices so every voice can be heard and your team meetings are at a time that works for the whole team.
- Problem-solve and strategize with your team.
- Have domain expertise.

Foundational to all of the skills above is the ability to listen and coach your team. Let's look more closely at coaching and how it differs from feedback. The other skills, such as trust, transparency, and caring will be fully explored in Part III.

Coaching

Coaching, as practiced by Michael Bungay Stanier in his book *The Coaching Habit*, tells us to stay curious a bit longer by asking clarifying questions and not giving in to the temptation to give advice. Asking good questions allows your team members to figure out a path forward on their own, so it's your job to ask questions that will get to that clarity.

Coaching is less about telling someone to do something but rather about asking great questions that enable them to uncover the best course of action. These questions also show you how your team member thinks and it can reveal blind spots that may lead to additional coaching or training. I learn about my team through having these coaching conversations. What's the issue? How have you tried to solve it? What do you think might work?

Asking questions is about being curious. After the question is asked, listen. Active listening seeks to understand first and foremost. Where is this person coming from? What's their perspective? It's hard to resist the temptation to give advice. Be quiet and listen carefully and ask follow-up questions based on what your seller is telling you.

These questions start with trying to understand in more detail what the seller's challenge is. Sometimes I note a pattern in their thinking and might express an observation. Sometimes my question might be prompted by reconciling what the seller is saying and what I see in a sales report. For example, they may want additional investment and tell me the deal size warrants that investment, yet when I look in the pipeline, their deal size is too small. So I'll ask questions to uncover what is really going on and assess the validity of the size of the deal. Ask open-ended questions, avoiding those that have yes or no answers. It takes practice to master this.

Feedback

The word *coaching* has many meanings. I often hear the terms *feedback* and *coaching* used interchangeably. They are different. Feedback is typically given when you are observing behavior of your seller that you deem to be ineffective or you are curious about. You may start out the conversation stating an observation you've had such as, "I'm observing that you are constantly late for our team meetings. Is something going on in your life preventing you from showing up on time?"

Other times the feedback may be based on concern for their results and pipeline health when you look at the sales reports. Or you may get feedback from colleagues. An example is the feedback that your seller is not collaborating. That feedback would prompt the need for a conversation with your seller to give them the feedback you received and ask for their perspective.

Ask questions. Listen. Foster an open communication channel with your team. These conversations are the basis for building trust. In *Dare to Lead*, Brené Brown writes, "Trust is built in the smallest of moments. It is earned not through heroic deeds, or even highly visible actions, but through paying attention, listening, and gestures of genuine care and connection." It is these small interactions that build trust. Ironically, trust can be broken much more quickly than built. Take care in your conversations with your team. You don't want to take trust-building for granted.

GROWTH MINDSET AND ADAPTABILITY

Employees require flexibility and managers must adapt. Flexibility requires empathy and understanding the seller's situation. Your conversations with your sellers are the foundation for building trust, understanding, providing feedback, and being empathetic. They are about building a relationship so that you can tackle the issues that come up and figure out how and when to make accommodations. They are also the foundation for creating a high-performing team, where your sellers want to work for you and they thrive and can do their best work.

One of my team members and his wife were expecting their

second child, and the team member wanted to take parental leave as is allowed through employee benefits. We had a conversation about leave and coverage for him while he was out. During this conversation, he shared with me that when his wife had their first child, he approached his manager at the time to talk about parental leave. That manager was not sympathetic to the employee or the benefits policies offered by the company and told him point-blank that to take the parental leave he was entitled to meant he really wasn't committed to his job. I was shocked. I dare say this approach does not help retain top talent.

The notion that work is just about work and personal lives are kept separate is another myth that's been chipped away at for decades. The COVID pandemic revealed the truth behind this myth. There is no separation of work or family. We are one whole being with many facets of our life to take care of. I mentor a woman who had to work remotely during the pandemic from the dining room table. Her three-year-old daughter, also forced to stay home, would come and sit on her lap while she worked. In many senses we know our team members more intimately now. We see inside their homes and see their families on video, even if only passing through a room. It is our job as managers to ensure we are supporting our team members to have the whole fulfilled life they require while delivering the results expected of them. It's invigorating and complex. Embrace it; it is not going away.

I've seen job descriptions with lists of skills and criteria so long that no living person on the planet can fill them all. These job descriptions discourage all but the brave few from applying. Maybe it is because of the tight talent market or the recognition that skills can be learned that I've seen a shift toward posting job descriptions with just the vital few skills and qualifications needed to do the job.

In the innovation economy and the current pace of change, what is relevant today will be obsolete tomorrow. It becomes critical to hire individuals who can learn, adapt, and grow as job roles inevitably change. Your role as a sales manager is ever evolving. You must adapt, learn, and grow alongside your sellers. Ever wonder why companies reorganize annually? Companies must evolve and change strategies to keep relevant and competitive. This is often seen as a disruption to team members. Being open minded and having a growth mindset has never been more important and is a foundational skill for all people in the workforce, manager or not. It becomes the role of you, the sales manager, to be able to explain organization changes and strategy changes.

This is why sales managers play the most important role in the innovation economy. We are all sandwiched between our companies' changing strategies and supporting the needs and changing expectations of our teams. We must navigate change and figure out how to deliver the results and revenue expected while retaining top talent and being the type of manager we and our teams want to work for. It's a big job.

The next section outlines the strategies and skills that will drive high performance as we move into the foundation of the Love Your Team system itself.

CHAPTER 2

The Love Your Team System

T he narratives we tell ourselves create our reality. We create new possibilities through conversations with others. When our narratives change, we change our world and what is possible. Your role as a sales manager is to interact with your team so they can be effective and deliver on what is expected of them in their role. On the surface, this may seem simple. Instead, it is complex and requires skill and forethought. Your interactions with your team happen through the conversations you have with them. Some may be written text and some may be verbal. You are responsible for the results of your team, both the good and bad.

If you're going to be a sales manager, you need collaboration and cooperation from your team. In essence, they need to grant you the authority to manage them. Why would they do that? You have the power to fire them. You control the resources. Given that you need them in order to be a successful manager, it is up to you to interact with them in such a way that they continue to grant you the authority to be their manager. You must build trust and a relationship with them. If you don't do this, they will leave your team and work for someone else.

The purpose of this chapter is to highlight that the actual work of being a sales manager happens for the most part in conversations. Conversations with your team, with colleagues, and with customers. Sure, there are follow-up actions you will take and pipeline analysis that you may do on your own. The real work of managing, though, happens in the conversations you have. That is what sales management is. I'll also introduce the categories of conversations that enterprise sales managers must master to be effective and why these are important to your success.

LOVE YOUR TEAM PRINCIPLES

When you accept a new sales management role, you most often will be managing a team that already exists. You will be the new boss. Sometimes people may join your team through a reorganization. The first order of business is to establish a relationship with your new team. How to do this is covered in the first series of conversations in Part II, called "Conversations of Connection."

The foundation of the Love Your Team system, and all of the conversations that make it up, is built on three principles. They are:

1. Trust—We must learn the skill of building trust with each person on the team. Our team will evaluate what we say and what we do and decide if we are trustworthy or not. Similarly, we evaluate our team. It is always good practice to assume trustworthiness until proven otherwise. Your

team will likely grant you provisional trust and it is up to you to maintain it through your words and actions.

2. Transparency—Part of building a relationship is being authentic and transparent with your team. They rely on you, the manager, to provide context for the changes happening at work. Context settles anxiety. It provides a narrative that gives perspective to emotions triggered by change. It can mobilize the team, provide excitement, or in some cases be interpreted as bad news. They want to know what is going on, whatever their emotional response, so they can adjust their expectations accordingly.

3. Caring—I say caring is foundational, but actually it is love that I mean. Caring is a way to show love. Caring is a word that is more acceptable in business, so I'm using it here. Care about your team and their interests. They need to know that they matter to you. They want to know that you will support them and have their back.

Making the Love Your Team system work depends on applying these principles in every conversation. It creates the environment to have the array of conversations outlined in this book.

THE FIVE CATEGORIES OF CONVERSATIONS

The seventeen conversation types discussed in Part II fall into five major categories. These are the conversations an enterprise sales manager must master to manage, retain, and support their team, and exceed their business and revenue targets.

Category 1: Conversations of Connection

These five conversations are about building trust and getting to know your team members more deeply. They form the foundation for human connection with your team. They revolve around understanding and supporting your sellers' needs, priorities, and career ambitions. These conversations establish and maintain your connection with each team member.

Category 2: Conversations of Performance

These conversations establish the goals and expectations for each team member. If a seller does not know what their sales quota is, it is hard for them to function or know what actions to take to overachieve. These four conversations also include establishing a regular review of progress toward goals, often called pipeline calls or deal reviews. Knowing how to effectively set, discuss, and manage performance expectations—such as sales forecasting, achieving revenue goals, building strong customer executive relationships, and securing resources to drive business results—gets results. Poor performance and performance coaching is covered. These are time-consuming conversations, but they are vital to you successfully creating and leading a high-performing team.

Category 3: Conversations of Strategy

These two conversations are all about coaching your seller and helping them refine their account plan, strategy, and deal pursuits. They cover how to navigate the landscape of complex enterprise deals and build stronger relationships with decision makers.

Category 4: Conversations of Customer Engagement

The main job of sellers is to be in front of their customers, increasing engagement, conducting meetings, resolving issues, and closing deals. But in reality, much of an enterprise seller's time and energy is spent preparing for customer-facing discussions with non-customer-related meetings and discussions. These three conversations revolve around customer connections, prepping for specific meetings, issue resolution, executive engagement, and what happens when something goes off the rails in the midst of customer discussions.

Category 5: Conversations of Internal Alignment

The three conversations associated with getting alignment within your company are covered in this section. For enterprise sellers, half their time is spent leading their internal teams and ensuring that their extended team is doing what's needed. In short, it's ensuring everyone on your side agrees, or is aligned, on the account strategy.

Selling is a team sport. There are numerous sales leaders and sellers who must work collaboratively in order to effectively sell complex solutions to enterprise customers. It is common for different views to surface and these need to be discussed and agreed upon so the entire team shows up coordinated and aligned in front of the customer. In some cases, team members will need to agree to disagree and then commit to a plan of action forward. In a large enterprise, it is not uncommon for 50 percent of a seller's time to be focused on ensuring internal team alignment and 50 percent of the time actually selling to the customer.

CONVERSATIONS LEAD TO RESULTS

Conversations are as much about building relationships as they are about business outcomes. It is not uncommon to have relationships with people you work with for thirty years or more. Relationships with work colleagues can create job satisfaction and camaraderie and make work more enjoyable. They are also about getting the work of business done, delivering business success. Business success enables all of us to take care of the things in life that matter: our families, friends, hobbies, travel, pets, etc. It is a virtuous circle, and conversations and human connection are the foundation.

All the conversations outlined in the book work together. You as the sales manager are creating a work environment of support and satisfaction that delivers results—work that works for your team.

How might one of these conversations show up in real life?

During COVID, I sent the following email. Members on my team were having a tough time. The pandemic had been going on for over a year and fatigue had set in. Stress was high. We were all tired of the blurred lines of work and homelife.

Email to My Sales Team

Subject line: Love Your Team

Hi all,

I realize this might be an odd subject for a work email. It came from a slide I used during a keynote address in July. I was speaking at a conference on the topic of hybrid work and what it means for sales leaders. I had a slide where I discussed strategies for talent retention and my first bullet point was, "Love Your Team." That phrase resonated with the audience. I talked about how managing a team needs to be personal and not just about work. Get to know your team and what matters to them and help them achieve it. The sentiment of love seemed most appropriate for how I feel about managing any team including this one.

I have been reminded recently by how present health and life challenges are for all of us in some form or fashion and how important it is to care for each other. This is still a tough time for many. It is harder to connect when remote. It is tough to know who needs extra understanding. I'd ask you to consider practicing being extra kind, empathetic, and patient. We still have a long road ahead before the pandemic ends and we settle into the next phase of hybrid work, and hopefully less stressful circumstances. We have members of our team who have had some tough situations over the past few months. It is a reminder to me that while we have work ambitions, nothing gets done unless we are OK and taking care of ourselves and each other.

- Last week, three of our team found themselves in a hospital emergency room for different non-COVID reasons.
- In the past two months, two of our team have had deaths in the family/extended family due to COVID.
- A few weeks ago, a coworker from the partner team committed suicide.

We are all in this together and please make sure you are taking care of yourself and those you love. Use the wellness days or step away. Ask for help.

Let me know what I can do to help or pitch in.

Thinking of all of you,

Helen

A number of team members let me know how much they appreciated this email and it reminded them that everyone has something going on, even if they don't know exactly what it is. It also had the effect of reinforcing with the team that family, health, and well-being come first.

The question for you, dear reader, is what will you do next? What type of sales manager are you and who do you want to be? How will you support your team, build trust, and retain your top talent? How will you maintain and sustain ever-increasing revenue expectations?

Are you ready to have these conversations with your team? The next part of the book shows you how.

PART II

THE CONVERSATIONS

♥

Conversations of Connection

As much as you want to work for Microsoft,
I encourage every employee to also
make Microsoft work for you.

—Satya Nadella, CEO, Microsoft

Your sales team members will commit, perform, and stay with you as soon as they succeed in making your company work for them. As long as they feel they are working for you and your company, they are at risk, and so are you.

As their manager, you are the connection point between each member of your team and your company's resources—products, processes, customers, goals, and capital. When you succeed in making and maintaining a meaningful personal connection with each team member—when each person feels you have their back—you strengthen their connection to their work, your company, and your shared mission.

Traditional sales managers minimize their personal connection with their team members. They take a transactional approach: the team member makes their number, they get paid, end of story. These types of sales managers are not focused on supporting their team members' careers or goals, just on making the number and being promoted to the next management role based on their sales success.

Conversations of connection always happen, even when they don't. They set the tone for the work environment, and if they are not happening or not happening constructively, that sets a tone too. Neglect them at your peril.

Love Your Team sales managers recognize that the bedrock of commitment, performance, and retention is human, not transactional. Employees are not machines that are easily replaced. For us humans, connections with other humans provide our purpose, drive, and meaning. These connections must be concrete and personal, not abstract, transactional, or functional.

Conversations of Connection depend more deeply than other conversations on the principles of trust, transparency, and caring discussed in Part I. Be prepared to be challenged by the temptation to apply the old traditions of sales management—skepticism, control, and valuing business results and transactions over people—as you work to master the foundation of the Love Your Team system.

This section explores the foundation of Love Your Team sales management. In it, you will find detailed guidance on how to prepare for, execute, and evaluate each of the five Conversations of Connection on which the Love Your Team system of sales management depends.

The five Conversations of Connection are:

1. Introducing Yourself to Your Team
2. Getting to Know Your Team
3. Maintaining and Growing Connections with Your Team
4. Developing Your Team
5. Amplifying Your Team's Success

CHAPTER 3

Introducing Yourself to Your Team

Traditional Sales Managers...	As a Love Your Team Sales Manager, You...
Tell the team what to expect. Talk about business priorities. Use "rah-rah!" to motivate the team.	Let the team get to know you as a person as well as your values, your leadership style, and what matters to you. Ensure each seller has the opportunity to ask questions and introduce themselves, depending on the size of the team, as an initial way for you to get to know your team.

PURPOSE

To introduce yourself to your new team. You want them to know you as a person, understand what matters to you, your leadership style, how to communicate with you, and your expectations of them. This conversation enables your team to briefly introduce themselves to you if the team is small, or at a minimum ask questions if it is not practical for each person to introduce themselves. It's an ice breaker that signifies the start of a new relationship.

INTENDED OUTCOMES

You put your team at ease. You create a favorable first impression with your team.

HOW TO RECOGNIZE THE NEED FOR THIS CONVERSATION

You become the manager of a preexisting team. This will likely be the case 95 percent of the time, rather than hiring and building your own team from scratch.

HOW TO DO IT

- ☐ Send out meeting/calendar invitations to your direct reports. Ideally this will be within one week of your new role being announced. I typically schedule forty-five minutes. This meeting could be in a conference room, remote using Teams or Zoom, or a combination of the two.
- ☐ Create a presentation about what you want your team to know about you. I make three PowerPoint slides:
    1. A slide about me
        a. Past companies and roles
        b. My family with photos
        c. Where I grew up

    d. A few of my favorite things: food, drink, places to travel

2. A slide communicating my management style. Mine reads:

    a. Clarity of objectives and goals

    b. Player/coach, empower the team

    c. Transparency

    d. Build & lead a high-performing team

    e. Culture & people first

    f. Available, text if you need help

    g. No surprises, communicate challenges early

3. A slide outlining the next conversation

    a. Getting to Know You, our initial 1:1 conversation. No preparation is needed. It's a conversation to get to know the seller better and learn what is top of mind for them.

    b. Maintaining and Growing Connections, through ongoing 1:1 conversations. It's your seller's time and agenda. Make the most of it!

☐ Conduct the team conversation. What I do:

1. I always turn on my video. No exception. I request them to do the same, although I don't force it if it is not comfortable for them.

2. If some sellers are missing, I record the conversation. If not, I don't.

3. I start by introducing myself and the agenda for the meeting. I will take ten minutes to let the team know

more about me, my style, and what to expect.

4. I ask the team to individually introduce themselves.
   a. Name, role, customer/territory, how long in the job/company
   b. Something more personal: What is your favorite food or place to travel? Or how do you like to spend your free time?

5. I close by communicating that I'm looking forward to getting to know each of them and I'm excited to take on this role. I let them know I'll set up 1:1 conversation times with each of them over the next couple of weeks to get to know them better. Instructions for the initial 1:1 conversation: just show up and have a conversation with me about
   a. Who they are
   b. What matters to them
   c. Their career goals
   d. Any challenges they want to share that I can support them through

ASSESSING IF IT WORKED

☐ Did all of your team join the call/show up for this initial team conversation?

☐ Were they interactive?

☐ Did they share something of themselves by way of introducing themselves?

☐ Did they ask questions?

All of these are good signs that your team is paying attention and are engaged. Do not fret if you cannot answer yes to all of these questions. This is your first conversation. There will be more.

THINGS TO CONSIDER

Sharing takes time, especially if you have a big team. You must facilitate the meeting to create balance between individual sharing and moving the meeting along.

I recently took over leadership of a thirty-person team. I invited everyone to this initial meeting. Instead of asking each team member to introduce themselves, I asked if there were questions or additional topics they were interested in discussing.

If you have a large team, setting up a meeting time that works for most of your new team can be a challenge. It is possible that this all-hands meeting may need to be scheduled out two to three weeks from your start date. In cases like this, what I do is begin having 1:1s with my direct reports as soon as possible and meet with extended team members (reports to my direct reports) over time. Having 1:1s with a thirty-person team can take two to three weeks to accomplish and I do not wait for the single larger call to begin.

CHAPTER 4

Getting to Know Your Team

Traditional Sales Managers...	As a Love Your Team Sales Manager, You...
Will focus their time initially on the business itself: customers, revenue, pipeline status and situation.	Understand that your team and people are your most important asset.
	Prioritize to meet your sellers (virtually or in person) within the first week of starting your new sales management role.
Will communicate performance expectations and what is needed in order to achieve the business outcomes desired.	Will focus on getting to know the seller: asking about their background, how long they've worked for the company, what matters to them, and their career goals.
	Realize learning the business will come.

PURPOSE

To get to know individual team members by inviting them to share more about themselves and any concerns or things they want you to know. To cultivate a successful team, you need to know how you can best support each member, and this begins with the initial 1:1 conversation, followed by regular checking in.

INTENDED OUTCOMES

You both understand more about each other. The seller asks questions as well as tells you about themselves. You open a channel of communication with your seller so they feel free in the future to seek you out when they have a problem, concern, or challenge before it turns into a bigger problem. Don't micromanage.

HOW TO RECOGNIZE THE NEED FOR THIS CONVERSATION

You are leading a new team. You have completed the initial team conversation.

HOW TO DO IT

☐ Send out a meeting/calendar invitation to each seller with a time and date that works for them. This may become a standing biweekly 1:1 meeting time with this seller, though it can be rescheduled when the need arises. Ideally, this first 1:1 occurs within one to two weeks after the team meeting. I typically schedule thirty minutes for 1:1s. This meeting could be in a conference room or remote using Teams or Zoom.

☐ Conduct the initial 1:1 conversation. What I do:

1. Invite the seller to share general info about themselves. The seller sets the agenda of what they want to share, but open-ended questions are good prompts:

   a. How are you doing?

   b. How's your family?

   c. Anything going on I should be aware of?

2. Ask questions about the seller's preferences and career goals. Here are some open-ended questions I like to use:

   a. What are your preferred working hours and availability?

   b. What are your preferred methods of communication?

   c. What are your career goals?

   d. How can I support your career goals?

   e. Is there anything regarding your current role that I should know about, i.e., pent-up issues or customer challenges?

   f. Is there anything I can do to help?

   g. Looking at the year ahead, do you have vacations or leave planned? Let me know with a meeting invite on my calendar so I know not to bug you during that time.

☐ Ask about biweekly 1:1 conversation frequency and scheduling. The seller may want more or less of these meetings. Subsequent 1:1 conversations may be more focused on particular goals or activities, but you'll always want to ask general questions.

☐ Share your own availability and preferred methods of communication.

ASSESSING IF IT WORKED

☐ Did your seller show up to their first 1:1?

☐ Were they interactive?

☐ Did they share something beyond what they shared in the team conversation?

☐ Did they ask questions?

Again, you are looking for engagement with you and an attempt to connect. Note: Everyone has different levels of engagement and preferences as to what and how much they want to share with a manager.

THINGS TO CONSIDER

Trust takes time. Approach employees with curiosity. Ask questions, listen, and learn.

CHAPTER 5

Maintaining and Growing Connections with Your Team

Traditional Sales Managers...	As a Love Your Team Sales Manager, You...
Don't ask. People are machines, after all.	Think of your sellers as humans with lives outside of work.
Need an in-person style of working.	Understand that your sellers have changing expectations and it is important to understand and do your best to accommodate those expectations.
Expect sellers to "always be on the job," be available to the boss when the boss wants to reach them, and prioritize critical work activities over vacations. If they don't, the seller is not committed to their job.	Recognize that your team is your number one customer and if you can't retain your top talent, it is tough, if not impossible, to achieve your business goals.

PURPOSE

To ensure you understand how the seller is doing personally and how they are progressing toward achieving their business goals. This is a forum for the seller to call out issues and ask for help as well as to highlight the great work they are doing. This is *their* time with you and *their* agenda. These conversations also enable you to understand where and how you can support them. For example, they may need help securing an executive for an upcoming customer meeting.

Conversations of maintenance, support, and growth build a relationship with the seller by showing them you care about their health and well-being. Knowing your seller better, in turn, informs future work planning and your coaching strategies. Over time, ongoing conversations also build a stronger, more trusting connection, which increases your seller's transparency and willingness to share.

INTENDED OUTCOMES

Your seller feels their work is workable and balances with their health, well-being, and family responsibilities. Ongoing 1:1s are about more than how a seller is feeling. They provide an opportunity to reinforce to your seller that you care and are here to support them. These 1:1s are also about business and progress toward achieving results.

You understand how the individual is doing, both personally and professionally. Are they on track with their goals? Are they meeting the expectations of the role? The 1:1 gives you an indicator of how that individual is performing in their role. Ask probing questions if you have concerns that the seller is not on track. These meetings also let you know where you can step in and provide needed support. This support may be to further a business outcome or to coach the seller when they are having a difficult situation at work.

HOW TO RECOGNIZE THE NEED FOR THIS CONVERSATION

These ongoing conversations with your direct reports should be held no less frequently than every two weeks. There are occasions due to travel or vacations where you might go a month between 1:1 conversations. This frequency will help you stay in touch and maintain a connection with each of your direct reports.

Employee health and well-being are the cornerstone of every conversation I have with my team. Physical and mental health are foundational needs. Whether it's their kids, partners, extended family, or pets, health and well-being always come first. Work will not get done to their best ability until health and family concerns are taken care of.

Maintaining a regular connection enables you to have a pulse on the business and address issues before they arise. Regular meetings enable you to ensure you are running a predictable and thriving business.

I target quarterly connection 1:1s with each skip-level (someone who reports to one of my direct reports) across the organization. Even that may not be feasible depending on how large your organization is. If it is not feasible, at least make a quarterly connection with your high-performing team members across your organization to support their career growth and tenure in your organization and at your company.

HOW TO DO IT

☐ Set a recurring conversation time for each seller. Mine are thirty minutes, biweekly, though they can always be rescheduled when the need arises. This conversation could be in a conference room or remote using Teams or Zoom.

☐ Conduct ongoing 1:1 conversations during the seller's regularly scheduled time. What I do:

1. Check in to see how the seller is doing. This part of the conversation is about their well-being and sometimes includes how their family is doing. This repeats what I do in the initial 1:1. The seller sets the agenda of what they want to share, but open-ended questions are good prompts:

   a. How are you doing?

   b. How's your family?

   c. Anything going on that I should be aware of?

2. During the meeting, the seller outlines their agenda for the call, the topics they want to discuss. I also share topics I want to discuss. We spend the next twenty minutes discussing the topics outlined. The majority of this call is likely to be focused on work-related activities and progress against goals. They may ask for help or extra support or funding for an initiative. I listen, take notes, and follow up if I have actions.

3. The types of topics my sellers often raise include the following. Many of these are covered in subsequent chapters in more detail. The ongoing 1:1 is often when issues are first raised.

   a. Upcoming customer meetings including executive meetings.

   b. Challenges or lack of alignment across the internal extended teams.

   c. Systemic gaps in resources and the impact on their sales efforts.

   d. Difficulty securing the right expert or resource needed to solve a customer challenge or address a customer request.

   e. Deal status and help needed.

   f. Informing me of a desire to interview for another role.

4. Check in to see if there is anything needed to ensure they are productive. This might include a change or update in work preferences.

5. Check in to see if they plan to take leave or vacation time. Here's what I like to ask:

   a. Looking at the year ahead, do you have vacations or leave planned?

   b. If the seller plans to take leave or vacation, I ask questions regarding when (this week, next month, this summer) and the duration (how many days, weeks, months). I also ask them to send me a calendar invite covering the time they are away. This ensures I know not to bug them during that time. I also ask them to track their time off in the time reporting tool. You or your company may have a different way of tracking an employee's time away.

c. If the team member has vacation or leave coming up within the month, I ask them to create a coverage plan that outlines what needs to be taken care of and who will take the actions needed to cover for them while they are out.

d. I ask the seller to review their plan with me at least a week in advance of their vacation or leave. This becomes one of the agenda topics for our 1:1 and we review the following:

   i. What customer-facing actions need to be covered while they are out and who do they propose to cover these? If they do not have a proposal, we discuss what to do. If there are areas of concern but not action, I expect the seller to highlight them. For example, there may be a customer escalation due to something happening while this seller is out.

   ii. What is the communication plan to the customer informing them that the seller will be out? Who will be the primary point of contact for the customer to reach out to if something is needed? I make every effort for that person to not be me. It is an opportunity for other members of the extended team to expand their scope of responsibility for a short period of time. I am often the escalation point noted on out-of-office emails, but I do not directly cover the seller's work unless there are no other logical options or it has customer executive involvement.

ASSESSING IF IT WORKED

- [ ] Is the seller comfortable sharing what is going on with them personally?
- [ ] Did the seller have an agenda for the meeting?
- [ ] Did the seller discuss what is top of mind for them?
- [ ] Did they come prepared to talk about the following:
  - [ ] How they are progressing against their goals?
  - [ ] The impact they are making in the business and with their customers?
  - [ ] Business challenges and help needed?

THINGS TO CONSIDER

I cannot overemphasize how critical these ongoing 1:1 conversations are. They form the basis for my relationship with each member of my team. These ongoing 1:1 conversations are where I learn what is going on with them, both personally and professionally. This is where I learn about an upcoming executive meeting or situations with a customer requiring my attention. This is where I assess my seller's progress against their work goals. This is often the time when they share with me their career interests or inform me of a job interview they are having within the company.

There has been a lot written recently about increased emotional anxiety and mental health issues, especially among early-in-career employees. Managers are often the first to spot changes in behavior, which could be a sign of underlying issues. According to Chester Elton, coauthor of *Anxiety at Work*, the best approach you can take as their manager is to gently state your observation that you have noticed a change in your seller's behavior and wonder if there is anything you can do to help.

Everyone needs time off and a break from work. Planning ahead can make your seller's time off less disruptive to you and enable others to step up and do more for a short period of time. This can be a career opportunity for those filling in for your seller temporarily.

CHAPTER 6

Developing Your Team

Traditional Sales Managers...	As a Love Your Team Sales Manager, You...
Focus on telling the team what to do, pushing their agenda, driving to achieve revenue/quota objectives.	Ask, "How can I support you?" Provide the opportunities and support for your sellers to fulfill their career goals.
See their relationships with their team as transactional and about doing stuff, not getting to know the team or caring what the team's career goals are.	Know that relationships are long term and that helping sellers' career goals pays off personally and professionally. This builds your reputation as a great manager to work for, thus making it easier to attract new talent now and in the future.
Attempt to block top performers from changing teams.	

PURPOSE

To support your seller's career development and progression. This typically means a promotion or another role within the company.

Increasingly, their career ambition may be broader and include an advanced degree, changing industries, or moving to a new country.

Encourage sellers to create a written career plan that they review with you quarterly. This provides a framework for determining the best actions (classes, on-the-job training, taking on stretch assignments, being mentored, job shadowing, etc.). It also enables you to support their plan and it becomes a record that documents plan progress.

If as is often the case they do not know how to create a plan, I offer a career plan template for them to complete prior to our next career discussion. It may be appropriate to just have an informal discussion on what they want to accomplish and the help they think they need from you. It is ultimately up to the seller to create and own their career plan and identify the resources and support needed.

INTENDED OUTCOMES

Supporting sellers' career goals and preferences increases job satisfaction, engagement, and talent retention. Top talent continually assesses whether or not the job, the manager, and the company are working for them and the life they want to lead. Another way of saying it: is the combination of work + compensation + life goals working for them?

Career development conversations serve to upskill and prepare sellers for the next step in their career. If the seller has ambition for a leadership position or a promotion within the company, building their personal brand and raising the visibility of their work and impact is most likely necessary. If I help them achieve their career goals, it is more likely they will stay working for me or the company. Keep in mind, not all career goals include being promoted; goals may also include moving into a different role within the company.

HOW TO RECOGNIZE THE NEED FOR THIS CONVERSATION

Make it a point to have a career development conversation once per quarter. Sometimes there is not much to discuss because the seller is not focused on their career. Other times, they are actively working the actions identified in their career plan and it is helpful to discuss progress, how it is going, and what modifications or new actions are needed.

This is a must-have conversation at least twice a year; four times a year is better. Sellers may ask for this conversation, but I recommend you just do it regularly.

HOW TO DO IT

Set up a recurring career discussion every three months for each team member. Ensure that the meeting invite denotes this as a career discussion. This conversation can be in a conference room or remote using Teams or Zoom.

☐ Have your seller share their career plan. My recommendation is that you provide a template where the answers to the questions below are noted and discussed. The career plan typically includes the following content:

1. Current role, years or months in role, and current job level (if your company has them).

2. What do they do well or like doing?

3. What do they want to do next?

4. What is the time frame to achieve this new role or promotion?

5. What knowledge and skills do they need in order to move into their stated career ambition (new role or a promotion)?

6. What actions are needed in order to obtain the desired knowledge and skills? Brainstorm with the seller opportunities available within the company, such as:

   a. Specific classes to take

   b. On-the-job training—be specific on what this entails, or who they need to work with to get this training

   c. Job shadowing—be specific on who to job shadow and what skills they hope to learn by doing this

   d. Specific books to read

   e. Mentoring to obtain skills—identify potential mentors; be as specific as possible

   f. Taking on new projects beyond their current scope of responsibilities

7. How are they interacting with senior leaders and peers?

   a. Suggest making a map of their network of connections within the company. The point of this is that it is often who they know, rather than just their skills, that will land them a new role.

b. Devise strategies for increasing their visibility with the people who are stakeholders in deciding promotions and/or new roles.

c. Coach sellers on relevant company politics and leadership structure that can help them be more effective.

8. What kind of assessments would be useful in determining competence and success? For instance, a 360-degree assessment in which their peers, managers, and customers provide input on their work performance. CliftonStrengths or Myers-Briggs assessments are also often used.

ASSESSING IF IT WORKED

☐ Did your seller create a career plan? Is it realistic and actionable?

☐ Do you have clarity on what you need to do to support their career ambition, if they have one?

☐ If your seller does not have a stated career ambition, schedule another conversation in three months to check in again.

THINGS TO CONSIDER

When a seller does not have career goals, it could be a sign that you have not earned their trust. Be aware that it may also mean that they've already decided to leave your team or company. You might ask your seller if there are reasons they would not feel comfortable sharing career goals.

I had a situation during a career conversation with an employee where they asked for a promotion. I told them that they were not ready for a promotion. I explained my reasoning. The seller disagreed. They subsequently showed me their work and invited me to meetings they led with their customer so I could see their impact directly. I agreed I had not had sufficiently deep conversations to elicit this level of detail. I was able to reassess the seller's merit after he gave me more evidence of his recent accomplishments and impact. I promoted him at the next opportunity.

The lesson: Learn from your mistakes and give your sellers the opportunity to prove you wrong when they disagree. Get curious and figure out how you missed their impact and correct it moving forward. Set up systems to understand in more depth how your sellers are performing. I often ask them to invite me to meetings they are leading so I can observe them in action. This helps me gauge their leadership and impact with customers and other team members.

CHAPTER 7

Amplifying Your Team's Success

Traditional Sales Managers ...	As a Love Your Team Sales Manager, You ...
Regard employees as workers to amplify the manager's success. They never consider what they can do to amplify the employee's success.	Ask, "What do you need?" Seek ways to support your sellers to ensure they show up strong. Empower your sellers to be the focus for delivering the result, not you.

PURPOSE

These conversations identify tasks you can do and resources you can provide to amplify your team's success. In short, these conversations show you how you can make your seller's job easier by taking actions often expected of a seller. This also serves to show that you are willing and able to do the jobs you ask your team to do. Through serving, you lead.

INTENDED OUTCOMES

Your team member feels increased support, satisfaction, trust, and loyalty.

HOW TO RECOGNIZE THE NEED FOR THIS CONVERSATION

This conversation typically has one of three flavors. The first flavor is there are tasks to be done, such as updating the pipeline when the seller is slammed and behind. If the seller and I have had sufficient conversations regarding the opportunity status, I offer to update the pipeline on behalf of the seller so they can focus on customer-facing activities that move the deal forward. This may also happen if I'm reviewing pipeline data and see that the seller has not kept it up to date. I just update it rather than bugging the seller for efficiency's sake. I always let my team know ahead of time that they may find that I've updated their pipeline on their behalf instead of micromanaging them to make sure it gets done.

The second flavor of this conversation happens when there is an important meeting where the seller needs to stay focused. This could be a customer meeting, or the seller is making a pitch for internal resources or deal concessions and is presenting the business case to our internal executive leadership who will decide the merit of the investments being asked for. In this scenario, we agree that I will take notes in the background during the conversation so the seller can focus on the meeting, presentation, or business case review he or she is delivering.

Last, there may be work needed to cover for a team member on leave or vacation. As part of the coverage plan, I may play a role in providing backup coverage if there are no other options.

HOW TO DO IT

☐ As part of your recurring 1:1 biweekly meeting, the seller will discuss important upcoming customer and executive meetings. The seller should know to include you in these meetings.

1. Discuss the meeting flow and ask if it would be helpful if you take notes in the background so they can focus won the discussion: being present, learning, and not worrying about capturing the follow-up actions. If they say yes, take the notes on their behalf. Whether or not you ultimately take the notes, always debrief these meetings when they are done and discuss effectiveness, what went well, what can be improved, and next steps.

2. If the seller is asking for deal concessions and customer investments or resources, you should be a part of the approval/review discussion and process. When the internal business case is being made by the seller, consider offering to take notes. The seller will then use your notes as the basis for the follow-up emails and actions identified during the meeting. I realize it

may seem odd that the seller is doing the business case pitch to the internal executive team. My philosophy is it is the seller's job to own the customer relationship and sales pursuit end to end and, as such, they need to own making the case for investments. I have also seen scenarios where the manager or a more senior executive in the seller's management chain will make the pitch. In this case, I do not take the notes; the seller would do that.

☐ Follow up with the seller during your next conversation to debrief the customer and executive meetings.

☐ As part of your recurring 1:1 biweekly meeting, check in on workload. With permission, I will sometimes add deal status notes after I speak with a team member.

☐ Discuss the updates done in the pipeline and discuss how the seller will fit pipeline updating into their regular workflow and day. This is a core expectation of the role, and while I may have jumped in and done it on the seller's behalf when they were pressed for time, it is expected that they will do their own updates regularly.

☐ As referenced in Chapter 5, I may step in and cover for them as part of their time-off plan. This is essentially me doing part of their job for them. This should be saved for only those instances where others on the team cannot fulfill what's needed.

ASSESSING IF IT WORKED

☐ When the seller was pressed for time, did they feel supported when I took on tasks?

☐ Did my note-taking in the background enable the seller to focus on their meeting or presentation?

☐ Did my involvement improve the overall outcome we were hoping to achieve?

THINGS TO CONSIDER

Don't let your willingness to jump in and help your team accomplish administrative tasks be a crutch for them. This should not be something they expect you to do. Chronic disregard for pipeline hygiene and updating may be a sign of a performance issue.

While I expect my sellers to run their customer meetings and pitch the business case for resources and deal concessions to internal executives for approval, I recognize that there are times when a seller may not be effective conducting these meetings. In this case and for the sake of the deal and progressing the customer relationship, I or another leader may conduct these meetings. In this case, I pivot to coaching and performance-managing the employee. It is core to a seller's role to be able to conduct these meetings.

Sellers should not rely on me to backfill them when they go on vacation. I expect them to have a plan as to who will cover for them.

SECTION 2

Conversations of Performance

Knowing how to effectively set, discuss, and manage performance expectations—such as sales forecasting, achieving revenue goals, building strong customer executive relationships, and securing resources to drive business results—gets results.

Addressing poor performance is equally necessary. Performance conversations also cover the hardest conversations: coaching underperforming sellers to deliver the results expected or move to a better-fitting role, and firing if necessary. Hiring and keeping a poor-performing team member is worse than having none at all. A poor-performing seller is like having a seller who is working for your competition.

As effective enterprise sales managers, we set, manage, and monitor the performance of our sellers. Most enterprise sellers are expected to deliver "hard" tangible results, such as revenue achievement, and "soft" results, such as securing internal resources effectively to support their sales pursuits and building strong relationships with their customers. Without providing clarity about performance expectations, it is unlikely the sellers will know the results they are expected to achieve.

Examples of hard results that can be measured:

- Revenue attainment
- Consistent forecast accuracy
- Growing share of wallet. This means increasing the percentage of the customer's budget they spend with you. Often this means that your competition has a corresponding decline.
- Consistent YOY revenue growth
- Maintaining pipeline and CRM data accuracy and pipeline coverage (3x is standard)
- Number of new customers signed (the New Logo metric), which is critical in the mid-tier space or when introducing a new product category
- Margin. Many, not all, sellers are measured on this.

Soft results come from taking actions that support the overall business but are not directly measured by revenue. Some of the performance expectations for soft results are assessed by observing behavior that supports the stated company culture and values.

Examples of soft behavior expectations:

- Building relationships with senior customer executives
- Expanding executive relationships across the customer's enterprise

- Creating a strong customer business plan and strategy (may include of both technical and business goals)
- Creating more value for the customer and articulating the value delivered by the seller's company
- Leading a strong cross-functional team and creating a healthy team culture
- Securing internal resources to advance your company's business with your customers
- Communicating effectively and demonstrating executive presence
- Ensuring business compliance and executing with integrity

Often, sellers operate as individual contributors in a matrixed organization where other team members from other departments —such as product specialists, technical sellers, and customer success sellers—are assigned to the seller's account. This extended team works collaboratively. Each of my team members is responsible for orchestrating that extended team, but everyone is a peer.

Clarity of expectations is foundational. In large enterprise teams, goals are created at a high level. Worldwide, all sellers are accountable for the same overarching quotas and behavioral expectations. Clear and monitored performance expectations keep the team working to deliver expected business results within appropriate behavioral and legal bounds.

Setting and communicating performance expectations—and holding sellers accountable—creates clarity. Expectations establish both the ends and the means. They also foster the three Love Your Team principles of trust, transparency, and caring.

The four Conversations of Performance are:

1. Setting Performance Expectations
2. Reviewing Pipeline and Forecasts
3. Keeping Performance on Track
4. Managing Underperformers

CHAPTER 8

Setting Performance Expectations

Traditional Sales Managers...	As a Love Your Team Sales Manager, You...
Evaluate performance by revenue attainment alone.	Set clear and specific outcome-based performance goals. These will likely include a combination of the following: revenue attainment, behavioral expectations, business growth, customer relationship growth, securing internal resources, and leading internal teams.
Provide no criteria for assessment of the seller.	
"Train" the seller using quick tips and tricks of cold-calling, product knowledge, negotiating, and closing the deal.	
Tell the team what to do and expect the team to do it, rather than flexing to enable each team member to be effective in a way that works for them.	Share domain expertise for pipeline and forecasting reviews.
Provide no conversations about predictable repeatable results.	Are invested in your team's success and provide feedback and coaching to boost team member performance.

PURPOSE

The first step to meeting expectations is to set them. I don't want ugly surprises—for me or my team—and I don't want any team member feeling uncertain on how they measure up to outcomes at any point in the process of working toward a quota. Pipeline forecasting, delivering revenue and quota targets, building strong customer executive relationships, behaving consistently with cultural expectations, and demonstrating impact and value-add to customers and internal team members are critical to creating clarity and setting a strong foundation for working effectively.

Setting and communicating expectations creates accountability and clarity for the seller. They know the results they need to produce to be successful and how that success is measured. They know the acceptable ways of getting to that success in terms of behavior. Expectations that are objective and transparent foster fairness, since everyone understands the goals and measures of success.

Company goals for the fiscal year tend to be overarching—for example, "achieve ten million in revenue." But these big goals are far from a SMART goal that breaks a goal down into something more tangible, something that is Specific, Measurable, Achievable, Relevant, and Time-Bound.

These conversations set expectations that help to clarify the smaller goals and activities needed to reach the big ones. My list of activities that need clear expectations are:

- Building pipeline that is three times the revenue target
- Forecasting accuracy of +/- 5 percent per quarter
- Increasing relationships with customer executives
- Strengthening team leadership
- Creating a strong account plan
- Keeping pipeline up to date and accurate

If you scaffold expectations within and for each activity, results for these activities and overall goals will be more consistent and on target.

INTENDED OUTCOMES

You achieve the organization's business goals for revenue, market share growth, and customer acquisition. Your seller creates deeper and expanded customer relationships and leads a strong account team. Seller satisfaction and engagement are increased. Your seller is set up for success.

HOW TO RECOGNIZE THE NEED FOR THIS CONVERSATION

At the start of the fiscal year, there are new business and revenue goals established and documented. When you take a new job and lead a new team, they likely will already have established performance goals. You may have the opportunity to provide input to performance goals or you may not. However, you will always have the expectation to monitor and manage the performance of your team, whether you've established their goals or not.

HOW TO DO IT

- ☐ Enterprise sales organizations will typically have a process where performance expectations are documented and discussed with the seller. This often happens at the start of the fiscal year.

- ☐ Seller prep: Ask your seller to articulate their high-level plan on what they will do over the next one to two quarters to achieve their performance goals. Discuss their overarching goals and their high-level plan during a thirty- to forty-five-minute meeting.

- ☐ After the meeting is conducted, add notes to the plan to further document your expectations based on your conversation or to clarify a performance goal.

ASSESSING IF IT WORKED

- ☐ Does the seller understand what is expected of them?
- ☐ Are the goals clearly articulated?

THINGS TO CONSIDER

It is critical that we document performance expectations. These will be formally revisited one or two times during the fiscal year. In addition to these formal reviews, there will be monthly forecast and pipeline review calls as well as biweekly 1:1s to checkpoint how the seller is doing and to provide course correction as needed.

CHAPTER 9

Reviewing Pipeline and Forecasts

Traditional Sales Managers...	As a Love Your Team Sales Manager, You...
Treat pipeline and forecasts as THE focus of performance.	Assess performance relative to expectations.
Pressure the team to optimistically forecast deals.	Expect pipeline transparency, revenue, and forecast predictability.
Let top performers run roughshod over the process and get away with not keeping the pipeline up to date.	Empower sellers to conduct sales pursuits according to the style and actions each seller believes are best.
Have massive forecasting and revenue unpredictability.	

(Table continued)

Traditional Sales Managers...	As a Love Your Team Sales Manager, You...
Will provide stories on how she or he progressed deals in the past and expects their sellers to progress deals in a similar fashion. Have last-minute "diving catch" wins or deals not in the pipeline come in and be celebrated. Create situations where sellers hide their true deals and pipeline to avoid deal scrutiny.	Hold sellers accountable to a tight forecast accuracy such as +/– 5 percent by quarter. Question last-minute wins as to why the seller did not have more deal control to anticipate the win within the quarter.

PURPOSE

To provide forecasting signals to the business of our anticipated revenues by month and quarter. This enables the CFO and executive leadership to model forward-looking investments and profitability, as well as to create business strategies to build a thriving, competitive, and high-performing company that maximizes investors' returns.

Forecasting predictability matters because without it, sales organizations will be under-resourced and lack the investments needed to optimize sales pursuits. Investments in enterprise sales organizations are tied to the predictability of revenue, which is identified through forecasting.

To keep everything on track, I will conduct pipeline reviews monthly or biweekly if deals are changing frequently or if it is the last month before a big deal is expected to close and there are a lot of little actions that must happen to get it over the finish line.

Because pipeline reviews and forecasting are so core to a seller's and sales manager's life, I thought it worthy to devote a whole chapter to this conversation. There is not anything particularly special about the Love Your Team approach when it comes to standard pipeline reviews and forecasting, although the frequency of reviews may be different.

INTENDED OUTCOME

Clarity of anticipated revenues and an assessment of risk of not making revenue targets. These pipeline review and forecast meetings enable us to "see the future" and set into motion actions to bolster revenue results and achieve performance expectations. This is where deal risk is identified and actions discussed to put deals back on track.

HOW TO RECOGNIZE THE NEED FOR THIS CONVERSATION

I am unaware of any sales organization that does not conduct regular pipeline and forecast reviews. It is a way for us to have insight into the validity of the deals in the pipeline and pipeline strength. It also enables us to assess how a seller is performing in building a strong pipeline and ask about specific actions being taken to progress deals to closure.

These pipeline and forecast meetings typically occur once or twice a month, depending on the volatility of the deals and the pipeline. It is common to have all the sellers on one call while each seller in turn goes through their top deals anticipated to close in the quarter.

HOW TO DO IT

Schedule meetings at a frequency needed to provide the revenue and pipeline insights needed. These meetings are typically Teams or Zoom calls. I recommend holding these meetings no less frequently than once a month.

☐ By seller, review the following:
   1. Seller's forecast of how much revenue they anticipate closing in the quarter. This might be a rolling three-month forecast or current quarter and next quarter. Each company will have its own standards. Typically, there is a worst-case/best-case and "closest-to-the-pin" forecast. Closest-to-the-pin is what the seller actually thinks will happen. Are there sufficient deals at the right level of maturity to support the seller's forecast?
   2. Seller's overall pipeline coverage. If a seller has a quarterly quota of $500,000, what is the total value of qualified deals in the pipeline? It is typical to use 3x pipeline coverage as a rule of thumb. Thus a seller would need a qualified pipeline totaling $1.5 million (3x of $500,000) expected to close within a quarter. Three-times pipeline coverage assumes that one-third

of the value of the deals in the pipeline will actually result in closed/won business for the quarter. If your close rate is higher or lower, you would adjust the pipeline coverage ratio expectation accordingly.

3. Top deals in the pipeline. Top deals may be the largest dollar deals or they may be the deals with the highest propensity to close, typically represented by being furthest along in the pipeline as represented by 60 percent or higher probability to close within the quarter. Or they might be deals tagged as "must win" for strategic reasons. This is when you would review the details of how the deal is represented in the pipeline and make sure these details are coherent:

   a. Are the notes complete and clear?

   b. Are next actions noted with due dates?

   c. Is it clear who owns each action required to progress the deal to closure? If not, what needs to happen to get that clarity?

   d. Does the seller need help? If so, what help is needed and by whom? For example, this could be securing, scheduling, and conducting an executive meeting with the customer's CFO.

   e. Is the revenue anticipated believable, understated, or overstated?

   f. Is the sales stage (20 percent, 40 percent, 60 percent, 80 percent) reflected correctly and aligned to the notes/actions?

g. Does the seller have a relationship and regular meeting cadence with the person who has the authority and budget to buy what is being sold?

ASSESSING IF IT WORKED

☐ Did the sellers attend the meeting and provide the details required for you to understand the deals in the pipeline, assess the performance of the sellers, and forecast revenue in the quarter and possibly next quarter according to the company's practices?

☐ Was the seller prepared to discuss the deal and next actions?

☐ Is the pipeline up to date?

☐ Does the seller have control of each deal and timing to close it?

THINGS TO CONSIDER

Over time you will understand the behavior of each individual seller. Some will understate the likelihood of their deals to close. Some will be overly optimistic. It is our job as managers to provide a revenue forecast that includes a roll up of the forecasts from our team along with our judgment as to what our best-case, worst-case, and closest-to-the-pin revenue results will be.

Every company and sales organization has expectations regarding forecast accuracy. We are expected to have a clear understanding of the deals our sellers are working to be able to forecast accurately with a +/– degree of tolerance.

Some deals may require a much deeper level of discussion than is practical during a forecast call. An action from the forecast call could be to have a subsequent meeting to figure out what needs to happen to unblock and progress the deal.

Some companies are using AI to forecast revenue and comparing the sales leader's forecast to the AI models. Over time, as AI models get better, it is possible that the CFO will use them to create the company's financial plan. Even if AI is used, I believe we will still need regular forecast and pipeline meetings. These meetings are THE mechanism we use to assess the performance of our teams in terms of ability to create new pipeline opportunities, progress deals through the pipeline, and predictably close deals.

I've heard futurists say that sales is a dying profession and one day, business buyers will use the internet and Google or Bing searches to find everything they need to know in order to assess products and services they want to buy. I don't believe this for a minute. The risk to enterprise buyers of choosing wrongly is too great. Those with authority to decide what to purchase, especially large-dollar-amount purchases, won't risk their careers on a bad decision. They will need to interact with humans—sellers—in order to mitigate the perceived risk of making a wrong decision. And just like an enterprise buyer needs a trusted seller to give them the knowledge and confidence to take that risk, enterprises themselves need the judgment of human beings—sellers and their managers— to confidently plan and manage their businesses.

CHAPTER 10

Keeping Performance on Track

Traditional Sales Managers...	As a Love Your Team Sales Manager, You...
Focus on pipeline, forecasting, and revenue as the sole criteria for seller performance and ignore how sellers get there.	Assess performance and address gaps in performance relative to expectations.
	Create opportunities and have a process to assess performance across all dimensions of expectations.
	Notice when a team member only asks about trivial aspects of the job in their 1:1s. This may be a sign that the seller is not focused on the right activities and outcomes.
	Prioritize top-performing sellers and find opportunities to highlight their results and how they achieve them.

PURPOSE

To ensure performance meets expectations across all dimensions of expected behavior and outcomes, it is critical to have an approach to determine how your team is doing. It is most common to checkpoint performance during regular 1:1 meetings with your seller. These 1:1s provide an opportunity for your seller to ask for help before a situation or deal goes off the rails. Equally, it is an opportunity for you to provide coaching to maintain performance *before* it declines to a level where a performance improvement plan (PIP) is required.

Many enterprise companies have required performance checkpoints that happen two to three times per year. While these are important for formal documentation on employee performance to ensure clarity of results to support promotions or PIPs, I find it is a mistake to wait for this formal process before addressing gaps in performance. My motto is that these formal checkpoints should not yield any surprises for my seller but rather reinforce messages I have already given.

There is a tendency to focus on underperforming sellers. This is a mistake. Your top performers deserve your top attention to ensure they are getting the support they need to excel. Amplifying their results can have an oversized impact. It also provides you the ability to highlight their great work, which builds their brand within the company and makes it easier for you to nominate them for awards and promotions.

INTENDED OUTCOME

Build a high-performing sales team. The seller meets or exceeds all performance expectations.

HOW TO RECOGNIZE THE NEED FOR THIS CONVERSATION

A regular cadence of formal and informal meetings sets predictable checkpoints for team members to report on progress and for you to provide coaching. Typically these conversations happen during regularly scheduled 1:1s. If performance is poor and needs addressing, these meetings will be more frequent, such as weekly. I'll talk about managing underperformance more extensively in the next chapter.

To aid in performance checkpoints, periodically solicit feedback from other managers or extended team members who work with your seller. This feedback provides the basis for coaching along with your direct observations of the seller's behavior and impact on the business, both positive and not so positive. Performance is a combination of tangible outcomes such as revenue closed, quota attained, and observed behaviors—measured against hard and soft expectations.

Behavioral expectations are aligned to the norms and behaviors associated with company culture and the specifics of the seller's role. For example, a senior seller may be expected to demonstrate the ability to lead an extended team of individual contributors who are assigned to support the customer and do not report directly to that seller.

When a seller is not meeting some aspects of their performance expectation, I repeat the expectation and try to help them understand its nuances.

HOW TO DO IT

☐ You already have your biweekly 1:1s scheduled. Use this time to checkpoint progress toward performance goals. This is a time where you provide feedback and coaching to the seller if you have any. If you have a performance concern, dig in more deeply. You may alter your biweekly 1:1 to a weekly 1:1 cadence to provide more time for deeper discussions on your seller's work.

☐ In addition to the informal 1:1s, there may be formal, company-mandated performance reviews. Each company will have its own cadence for formal performance reviews.

☐ Manager prep: Create opportunities to see your seller in action by attending executive meetings they conduct, quarterly customer business reviews, and internal presentations where they are making a business case for investment and resources.

☐ Team member prep: As part of normal biweekly 1:1s, expect your seller to be prepared to discuss their progress toward goals along with challenges they are having.

☐ Follow up: If you continue to have performance concerns, ask your seller to send you examples of work products and insist that they include you in meetings they are conducting with their customer, extended team, or company executives so you can get a clearer picture of how they are conducting themselves and moving the business forward.

ASSESSING IF IT WORKED

- ☐ Is the seller making progress toward meeting or exceeding all performance goals?
- ☐ Does the seller understand what is expected?
- ☐ Is the seller being forthright and transparent? Are they providing opportunities for you to see them in action when meeting with their customer?
- ☐ Does the seller have clarity on actions they are expected to take?

THINGS TO CONSIDER

You have to know where you are so you can course correct if needed. But you also have to know how to balance between too much oversight, which leads to micromanaging and time being sucked away with meetings, and too little oversight, where the team may be underperforming without it being addressed. Most of the team's time should be spent selling, so give them the space to sell.

Keep your own time in mind. A team of twelve to fifteen enterprise sellers is about the limit that can be managed with the attention needed to coach the team for high performance.

CHAPTER 11

Managing Underperformers

Traditional Sales Managers...	As a Love Your Team Sales Manager, You...
Are dismissive when a team member is not meeting expectations. They take actions to get the team member to quit without having to do the extra work required to put them on a performance improvement plan.	Address performance issues head-on with the underperforming seller.
	Are not afraid to have the tough and often uncomfortable conversations required for improvement.
Ratchet up the pain so an underperforming team member will leave on their own, such as by increasing quota, assigning them to stagnant customers, or ignoring them.	Create a performance improvement plan with clear, bite-sized goals and expected outcomes.
Pass on sellers with performance issues to other managers by obscuring those issues and highlighting why the seller will do great on another team.	Set up weekly 1:1s to assess incremental progress against performance goals specified in the plan.

(Table continued)

Traditional Sales Managers...	As a Love Your Team Sales Manager, You...
Create a performance improvement plan that is unrealistic and designed for the underperforming seller to fail. Use it as a setup to push that seller out.	Provide feedback and coaching during weekly 1:1s to help the seller course correct so they can be successful achieving the plan goals.
Are not invested in their sellers. Sellers are a tool to be used and discarded if they don't work out.	Work with HR or senior leadership to terminate an employee when there is clear evidence they are not performing to the expectations of the role.
Don't communicate objective measurements or conduct conversations on what needs to improve.	

PURPOSE

To address the gaps you've identified in performance and give the seller the opportunity to demonstrate that, indeed, they are able to perform to expectations. This is done by meeting with the seller, communicating those gaps, and setting clear short-term goals that enable the seller to demonstrate improved performance.

These conversations provide a structure to assess performance improvement and monitor progress through weekly 1:1s. At this point, it is critical to have clear, actionable goals and document performance through these weekly meetings.

Unlike the initial setting of expectations, which is preventative care, and monitoring performance along the way, which provides maintenance feedback and mild course corrections, PIPs address specific symptoms of a now seriously "sick" performance.

I won't lie. These conversations are tough, unpleasant, and often lead to a seller feeling betrayed and misunderstood, at least at first. Addressing underperforming sellers is vital to building a strong team culture and creating a high-performing team. Left unaddressed, other team members will start feeling resentful as they may be overfunctioning to fill gaps created by the underperformer. Additionally, top performers may lower their performance if they believe there is little reward for maintaining high performance. They may even decide to leave your team.

INTENDED OUTCOME

Create clear evidence as to whether the seller who is on a PIP can deliver to the expectations of the role.

It is always desirable for a team member to improve performance and be retained in their current role. This does happen. I've had team members course correct even in dire-looking situations. However, it is rare. In my experience, most who start a PIP and have great skills will move into a better-fitting role before concluding the PIP. This is a fine outcome. We want our sellers to be in a role where they can succeed and do well at the company.

Many sellers starting a PIP don't have sufficient transferable skills to land a new role in a timely fashion. Or there may be a hiring freeze and new roles are not available. These sellers will end up concluding their PIP without demonstrating improved performance. Their employment will end. Often, they will find a new job outside the company on their own and resign. In other cases, their employment must be terminated for cause.

HOW TO RECOGNIZE THE NEED FOR THIS CONVERSATION

A seller does not meet performance expectations. You have probably received feedback from other team members or managers that your seller is failing to meet certain expectations of the role. Negative feedback from others and/or gaps in delivering expected outcomes could be indicators of underperformance. More digging is needed to really uncover what is going on and to double-check these reports.

As the manager, I often am not close enough to the day-to-day activities to observe my seller in action and I need to learn more. I need objective evidence.

So I get curious. I gather a range of nuanced feedback from peers and other managers and hard data from reports to objectively show which areas the seller needs to improve. It's crucial to not jump to conclusions before approaching the seller, as trust and transparency need to be maintained, especially in these delicate conversations.

I also get information from the seller's point of view. I spend more time with the seller and will create a plan that gives the seller the opportunity to show me they can indeed do the role as defined. At this point, I consult with HR and follow the company-prescribed guidance on handling underperforming employees. I always want to create a PIP that clearly documents expectations and tracks progress toward meeting them. This ensures my ability to terminate the seller's employment later or take them off the plan. The plan enables me to see more clearly what is going on with the seller so I can assess gaps and provide coaching and support for any needed improvements. As stated previously, I do not micromanage. I need to get closer to the situation to really understand it and tailor my support to be minimally invasive but still effective.

I had a seller who was treating team members as subordinates and was characterized as controlling the information flow across the team and with the customer. This leadership style is inconsistent with the trust, respect, and transparency that is part of the cultural expectation of the job. I worked with this individual to change their approach. They created a plan of action to rebuild trust and create a strong team culture where every team member felt valued. It was hard work, but over time, this team member ultimately changed how they led and interacted with their team, empowering each member to own their own deal pursuits and customer engagement activity. This change of approach freed up my seller to focus on building stronger executive relationships by shifting from being involved in all deal pursuits to checking deal status with the team to make sure they were on track.

HOW TO DO IT

☐ Set up weekly 1:1s with underperforming sellers to go over performance. This meeting could be in a conference room, conducted remotely, or hybrid.

- ☐ Create a PIP outlining performance goals to be achieved over a six-to-eight-week period, which would demonstrate that the seller is meeting expectations. Note that for more senior employees, I will outline specific outcomes I want them to achieve and ask them to create a six- to eight-week PIP with clear weekly goals.
  - ☐ It is common in larger companies to consult with HR before presenting the PIP to the seller. Every company has their own approach.
- ☐ Seller prep: Come prepared to discuss progress against weekly performance goals.
- ☐ Conduct the 1:1 conversations:
  1. Create or review the PIP. Define behavior and outcome expectations for the specific area that needs improvement, lay out the activities that will demonstrate this improvement, and define how you as a manager will assess progress.
  2. Assess if they did or did not reach the prior week's goals.
  3. Set activity and outcome expectations for the following week.
  4. Provide feedback and coaching to the seller during the weekly conversation.
- ☐ Follow up: After the 1:1 weekly meeting, formally document the conversation with the seller including progress toward and gaps in meeting the PIP goals. Endeavor to communicate verbally first what you will put in writing. There is a

temptation to "be nice" during the meeting and then provide negative feedback in writing.

ASSESSING IF IT WORKED

- ☐ Has the seller delivered against the specific goals as set out in the PIP? If so, they can be taken off the PIP.
- ☐ Does the seller realize that they are not a fit for their role and decide to move to a better-fitting role in the company, or resign from the company?
- ☐ Did the seller fail to meet the specific goals of the PIP? If so, this often sets into motion your ability to terminate their employment. Consult with your HR team on next steps.

THINGS TO CONSIDER

In my experience, if something seems off, it is worse than I realize. Is this a failing on my part as a manager? Maybe. I assume and believe everyone can perform until proven otherwise. So I sometimes miss underperformance and it goes on too long. I've also experienced the opposite situation in which a team member asked for a promotion and I did not think they were performing at a high enough level to warrant it. They proved me wrong. Again, this requires more intentional management conversations to understand the actions behind the results.

Many companies use a PIP that documents performance gaps, actions expected, and progress achieved. It also serves to put the employee on notice that their performance must change in specific areas and failure to demonstrate that change will likely result in employment termination. Whatever approach your company uses, make friends with HR. They will help you navigate the difficult landscape of addressing underperforming sellers.

SECTION 3

Conversations
of Strategy

I f you don't know where you are going, any road will take you there.

This section is all about coaching your seller and helping them refine their account plans, strategies, and deal pursuits. These conversations happen as a natural course during your 1:1s with your team. If there is a particularly sizable and complex deal being pursued, you may opt for weekly 1:1s to ensure you are deeply engaged in supporting your seller to close the deal. It is important that your seller review their key deals with you regularly. Inevitably they will need your support and approval for certain portions of the deal pursuit process, such as approving investments required to get the deal closed.

There are other forums for discussing account and deal strategy where extended team members and other managers are involved. These conversations are covered in subsequent chapters in Section 5, Conversations of Internal Alignment.

I've found that sellers benefit from brainstorming their account strategies with me. I can often provide them with resources and input they may not have considered. This is where having a large network and experience in the industry pays off.

One of my favorite parts of being a sales manager is discussing account strategy with sellers and ideating on the pros and cons of selecting paths to move a deal forward. For example, do we need to introduce a reference customer or navigate the complexities of getting a preview of the product roadmap? Do we need to propose a proof of concept so the customer can validate that the solution works in their environment? If so, are we clear on the customer's buying criteria and can we get them to sign a deal in advance that stipulates that if the solution meets said criteria, they will buy?

There are always many facets to a customer's internal political landscape, as well as the complexities of getting internal alignment to support the deal we want to present to the customer. All of these require conversations around account strategy and deal coaching with the seller. Sellers need to have a manager they can talk to without judgment or recrimination when they get stuck and need help considering alternative approaches to a challenge.

Conversations of Strategy are intended to help your seller think through challenges they are facing at an account or deal level. They include ideation and problem-solving: ideas and actions the seller can use that produce the outcome they are seeking with the customer.

The two Conversations of Strategy are:

1. Securing Executive Sponsorship—Creating strategies for building stronger relationships and value with customer's C-level executives. Identifying appropriate internal executive sponsors to pair with key customer executives and then figuring out how to have your internal executives agree to be executive sponsors.

2. Helping Your Team Get Unstuck—This is a catch-all for the varied challenges your seller needs help with.
   For example:
   a. Getting to the right person within your organization who can say yes to a request; an example would be approval to disclose a product strategy and roadmap plan.
   b. Figuring out how to answer the varied customer requests that come in.
   c. Strategizing on how to address difficult team dynamics.
   d. Brainstorming how to gain access to customer executives to build stronger relationships and value across a customer's organization. Given the complexities of enterprises, reporting relationships are often unclear and customers reorganize frequently making it necessary to rethink engagement strategy. Often this conversion includes the question, "Who do we know that knows the new person in charge of a key department at the customer?"

CHAPTER 12

Securing Executive Sponsorship

Traditional Sales Managers...	As a Love Your Team Sales Manager, You...
Do not spend time coaching their team on how to effectively engage customer executives.	Have domain expertise on the product and service that your team sells. Know what it takes to sell your products and services. Spend time with your sellers, coaching and strategizing.

PURPOSE

To help sellers think through how to build stronger relationships with customer executives. These could be line-of-business, C-level, IT, or other departmental executives. Often this conversation centers on one of three things: identifying who would be a great executive sponsor from your company to be paired with the customer executive, determining what executives in your organization have expertise that would motivate the customer executive to take a meeting, and finding out who we know that knows the customer executive.

INTENDED OUTCOME

The seller sees new actions they can take that progress toward their goal of building customer executive relationships and deepening their understanding and influence in the account. The outcome is that your seller gains access to a customer executive they've not met and who is interested in meeting with someone from your executive team. This access may uncover new opportunities or move an existing one forward. The fundamental expectation is that your seller is building relationships with relevant customer executives.

Examples of this are pairing your corporate vice president who has deep technical knowledge with the customer's chief information officer, or pairing your human resources executive with the customer's human resources executive.

HOW TO RECOGNIZE THE NEED FOR THIS CONVERSATION

A seller may be stuck or uncertain and proactively seek help. This troubleshooting conversation comes up when a new customer executive relationship is needed. For example, an executive sponsor is leaving your company and you need to find a replacement. Uncovering this problem often happens in biweekly 1:1 conversations when you check in on your seller's progress against goals.

It is an expectation for sellers on my team that they are always building stronger relationships with their customers, including getting higher in the organization. I periodically ask the seller how this is going, which prompts this discussion.

HOW TO DO IT

- [ ] These conversations are held during the biweekly 1:1 unless a special need arises that triggers an out-of-cycle conversation. This may be in person or remote.
- [ ] The conversation consists of brainstorming ideas and providing the seller with approaches to engaging with customer executives. It is common that a seller will not have enough seniority or strong enough relationships with the customer to get a meeting with the executive by themselves. This is where having "bait in the bucket," a senior executive or someone with domain knowledge of interest to the customer executive, becomes necessary. It is often nontrivial to get an appropriate executive engagement lined up, and the seller will often need help or, at a minimum, need to brainstorm ideas. Strategize on how to identify and approach the right internal executive, including the specific request and time commitment involved.
- [ ] One avenue for building executive relationships is to invite relevant customer executives to CEO, CIO, or other executive forums. The seller is not invited but will then have the opportunity to follow up with the attending executive. Executive briefings are another excellent way to build stronger relationships with more senior executives.

□ Follow up: Check in on actions taken and progress that is made or not made. Provide additional coaching if needed.

ASSESSING IF IT WORKED

□ Did the seller take action?

□ Does the seller need additional coaching on further action?

□ Does the seller now have new relationships with relevant customer executives?

□ Is there an internal executive sponsor assigned to your seller's accounts?

THINGS TO CONSIDER

Everyone is busy. Executives are busy and are picky about who they spend their time with. It is not trivial to build strong relationships with customer executives. When they are in place, it can be magical in terms of business insight and mutual value achieved. When a seller who has developed these relationships leaves an account, it can take a couple of years to rebuild those connections, and that assumes a talented seller takes over the account. Losing top talent and the relationships they've built has a negative impact on revenue. Customers hate "training" new reps assigned to them. A new rep assigned to an established account will need support from you as their manager to build customer credibility, especially if the account isn't covered by an extended team that already has multiple relationships. Attrition hurts customer satisfaction.

CHAPTER 13

Helping Your Team Get Unstuck

Traditional Sales Managers...	As a Love Your Team Sales Manager, You...
See what they can get out of the customer. It's about the largest revenue deal possible, not long-term relationship building or customer value creation.	Spend time coaching your team.
	Focus on delivering durable customer value and relationships with your customers.
Do not build trust with customers. Customers buy because they have to, not because they want to.	Understand the need to work collaboratively with colleagues.
Think that account and deal coaching consists of telling stories about how they won big deals in the past and therefore believe the seller should do the same.	Assist team members with problem-solving and strategizing.
	Make yourself available to coach your sellers and see coaching as central to your job role.
Leave the seller to strategize alone.	
Tell the seller what to do.	

PURPOSE

To help your seller figure out the best approach to move forward when they are stuck. You do this primarily by asking good questions. Of course, there are times when you know relevant facts or resources that they do not know, which can be helpful to share with your seller.

Conversations surrounding ideation, strategy, and coaching help your seller figure out the resources that can be used for maximum impact and clarify the customer situation.

This is general coaching and a myriad of topics may arise, such as who to speak with to get a customer invited to a conference, how to address nuanced relationship challenges across the extended team, or addressing a customer's specific request. These conversations help your seller network internally, helping them figure out which peers and executives would be most useful in a particular customer meeting.

These conversations also present a fantastic opportunity to better understand the seller's deal strategy and, importantly, is often an opportunity to tell them what a great job they are doing and how much you appreciate their contribution. While your coaching is valuable when they are stuck, it is also critical to find ways to let your seller know how great they are doing when they are doing great things.

INTENDED OUTCOME

Your seller is able to problem-solve quickly and get into action. Being able to seek coaching and have clarity as to how to move forward removes friction from your seller's day-to-day job with the customer.

Ultimately, these conversations help your seller get better business outcomes, such as shorter sales cycles, increased revenue, improved customer executive engagement, and less friction in deal pursuit.

Your seller sees the action that needs to be taken to unblock what is stuck and takes that action. Your seller resolves their challenges, their opportunities progress in the pipeline, and they achieve or exceed revenue quotas and other goals. Sellers who are doing a great job feel appreciated.

HOW TO RECOGNIZE THE NEED FOR THIS CONVERSATION

These conversations often happen naturally in deal coaching and status reviews in biweekly pipeline calls. I ask questions and, based on the responses, I provide additional coaching that is specific to a deal or customer situation. Pipeline reviews occur in addition to 1:1s, with eight to ten people on the calls. During pipeline review calls there will inevitably be deal coaching and discussion on how to progress a deal. This is discussed in more detail in Chapter 9: Reviewing Pipeline and Forecasts.

In general, these conversations focus on business pursuits that are stuck. For example, a seller may not know who to go to for help. As a senior sales leader with thirteen years of developing connections across Microsoft, I often have more knowledge of the people and resources to utilize than my seller. Facilitating these connections also expands my team members' networks within the company.

Another example of a situation that triggers this category of conversation is a customer wanting your company to sponsor their charitable event. The seller asks, "Who needs to approve this?" Often the budget and approval is not within the sales organization.

Another example is a new senior executive has been hired in your company and wants to meet with your customer executives. Essentially, they want an introduction to your customer. A conversation with your seller needs to happen to discuss the pros and cons of this. Will the newly hired executive add to the existing relationship? What is their role? What do they bring to the table that would compel a customer executive to want to meet with them?

One more example is when the seller is trying to break into a customer division they've not worked with before. They need help figuring out the best way to approach that challenge. Sometimes these conversations are centered on progressing a specific deal and the seller is looking for ideas and coaching because something is blocked.

HOW TO DO IT

- ☐ These conversations happen during 1:1s. The biweekly 1:1 is where they happen most often. Sometimes there is a need to meet quickly and you will need to set up a one-off 1:1 to discuss.
- ☐ A seller raises a customer engagement issue during a pipeline review or biweekly 1:1.
- ☐ You see an issue that needs addressing and you raise it during a scheduled 1:1 or request a one-off discussion.

☐ You discuss the issue with your seller. You ask questions to understand what is really going on. Resist the temptation to give advice. You do not know the customer situation as well as your seller does. Instead you explore pros and cons of different approaches. You continue discussing the issue until your seller has figured out how to move forward.

ASSESSING IF IT WORKED

☐ Did your seller figure out what to do to get unstuck?

☐ Did your seller take the actions needed to move forward?

☐ Is your seller feeling unstuck?

☐ Did your seller get their desired resolution to their situation?

☐ Are the affected opportunities progressing in the sales pipeline?

☐ Did you express your appreciation to your seller for doing great work?

THINGS TO CONSIDER

Keep in mind, 95 percent of what a seller talks about is based on their knowledge of the customer. I rely on the seller to know what's going on. Even if I've covered an account before, situations change over time. I get the general picture of the account through annual reports and customer meetings I attend, but I get the nuances through conversations with my seller. I trust my seller to understand how their customers are structured, who's in charge, and what their real business goals are. Sellers are the true navigators of their accounts.

I am there to ask questions, help troubleshoot why an account is stuck, brainstorm strategies that enable my seller to move forward, and learn what my seller is doing well and appreciate them for that.

Helping your seller get unstuck often includes navigating internal politics or bringing in outside resources such as third-party partners. Your seller may not be aware of internal political land mines or partner capabilities that you can make them aware of as part of the conversation.

SECTION 4

Conversations of Customer Engagement

The main job of sellers is to be in front of their customers, increasing engagement, conducting meetings, resolving issues, and closing deals. But in reality, much of an enterprise seller's time and energy is spent *preparing* for customer-facing discussions with non-customer-related meetings and discussions.

Customer meetings have multiple flavors. There are the day-to-day selling and relationship-building meetings with customers, some casual, others more formal. There are executive briefings where strategy and direction are discussed. And there are quarterly or semi-annual business reviews.

Day-to-day meetings are often part of deal pursuits and may require special briefings such as product roadmap discussions. In some cases the seller has established a monthly product update cadence so the customer can stay abreast of new offerings.

Other types of regular customer meetings focus on topics such as the customer's business strategy and how solutions and future solutions may be a fit, and specific challenges that are preventing the customer from realizing the value of what they purchased. These meetings can lead to other types of conversations with customers to pursue those specific opportunities.

Quarterly business reviews are more formal meetings with the customer and discuss your current business with the customer, changes to the customer's priorities and organization, and what's working and not working. These quarterly reviews help both companies stay focused on the priorities that matter most to the customer and give you an opportunity to address concerns before they fester.

Many of these meetings are conducted by extended team members in addition to the seller. In a complex enterprise, it takes the extended team in coordination to understand the customer and uncover opportunities for future business.

To meet the needs and issues of customers, sellers must mobilize internal teams and resources. Internal alignment is the name I give to the activities and meetings focused on gaining agreement within my organization on strategies, investments, and resources needed for my customers. It gets back to why sellers spend half of their time focused internally, with the goal of creating alignment across internal teams, as will be discussed in Section 5, Conversations of Internal Alignment. Customer-facing selling is just one piece of the job. If you can't mobilize internal resources and sell within your own company, you're less valuable to customers. It's a core skill for sellers to build networks and relationships, and it takes savvy and skilled conversations to know what people and resources are available to bring to bear for their customers.

Therefore, it is critical to gain support and agreement from leadership teams and individual contributors on the extended sales teams who must collaborate on account strategy, solutions, offerings, and customer success. Additionally, these conversations ensure we run the sales plays expected by the organization.

This is all for the sake of building a strong pipeline, addressing customers' business challenges, and generating revenue. The actual time spent with customers somehow gets truncated in the midst of all of this coordination inside our own organizations.

And no matter how you might prepare, there will always be a hiccup that causes a customer issue: an outage, a tech glitch, delays in discount approvals, a pandemic, a war.

Discussing with your seller how to address customer issues and effectively escalate to management can reduce the negative impact of all customer issues.

Addressing customer issues is different from other conversation categories because these conversations do not happen day to day, but they are important. I am an escalation point for customers. Conversations happen between combinations of stakeholders to get issues solved—seller to sales manager, seller to customer, sales manager to executive team. The permutations are many, and many conversations may occur before the issue is finally resolved.

This section discusses the crucial conversations and skills needed for coaching sellers to prepare for and conduct effective customer meetings and handle customer issues. As sales managers, we want our team members to feel supported and know we care about them individually and have their back if needed. As I've said in earlier chapters, support increases job satisfaction, effectiveness, and engagement.

When we support our sellers, they can support their customers.

Customers feel valued when they are supported. A valued customer gives the seller the opportunity to deliver more value and satisfaction, especially when issues are addressed quickly and effectively. Customers want to be heard and for steps to be taken to lessen the chance of any problem happening again. Ensuring customers feel that sellers and their managers understand their business needs and support them through trouble builds even stronger trust and value. Failure to address customer concerns causes multifaceted issues, from a customer requesting a seller to be removed from their account, to losing business, to ultimately losing that customer.

The three Conversations of Customer Engagement are:

1. Preparing for Customer Meetings—These are the conversations you have with your seller to prepare for a customer meeting. You and your seller will discuss the purpose of the meeting, who is attending from their side and yours, and what issues are likely to be brought up. What outcome is the seller looking for as a result of the meeting?

2. Preparing for Executive Meetings—These are meetings where your executives meet with customer executives. It could be a quarterly executive sponsor touch-base, or it could be your CFO talking to their CFO, or it could be your product executive meeting with the customer to address product issues or product strategy concerns.

3. Resolving Customer Issues—These conversations are triggered by a customer issue or escalation. For example, there may have been a recent outage or product support issue. Or the customer does not like a proposal they received, or the customer perceives we've promised something that we cannot deliver in the committed time frame.

CHAPTER 14

Preparing for Customer Meetings

Traditional Sales Managers...	As a Love Your Team Sales Manager, You...
Own, attend, and take over customer meetings and negotiations. Leave it to the seller to prepare for important customer meetings.	Support and empower sellers to own and run customer meetings. Coach sellers to maximize the chance of obtaining desired business outcome. Attend but do not own or run critical customer meetings.

PURPOSE

To prepare the seller for high-stakes customer meetings in which key issues are discussed and actions identified to move mutual business priorities forward. You and your seller will discuss the purpose of the meeting, its agenda, who is attending from their side and yours, issues likely to be brought up, and the outcome the seller is looking for. You should also use these conversations to understand the role your seller wants you to play in the meeting.

INTENDED OUTCOME

The seller goes into the customer meeting prepared and confident. The meeting runs smoothly with good time management and no surprises. The business outcome is realized. The customer meeting ends with a clear set of actions and next steps, including scheduled follow-up meetings.

HOW TO RECOGNIZE THE NEED FOR THIS CONVERSATION

There is an upcoming high-stakes customer meeting. It is important to ensure you and your seller are aligned on the agenda, purpose, and outcomes you both want to achieve in that meeting.

HOW TO DO IT

There are two aspects to discuss here: 1:1 meetings with your seller in preparation for the critical customer meeting and actually conducting the meeting with the customer.

1:1 meeting prep with your seller for high-stakes customer meetings:

- ☐ Discuss the upcoming customer meeting during a biweekly 1:1 or set up another time dedicated to this discussion.
- ☐ Seller prep: Come prepared to discuss the customer meeting's agenda, purpose, intended outcome, participants, content, and potential issues that could arise.

☐ Ask questions and discuss topics from your seller's prep. Questions include: Who are you going to invite from our side and why? What customer concerns are likely to be brought up? What role does your seller want you or other internal execs to play?

☐ Your seller will review the PowerPoint slides they have prepared for the customer meeting. You provide feedback. Depending on the significance of the meeting, you will likely meet at least twice with your seller to prepare. Your seller will update their PowerPoint slide deck before each review with you.

Conducting a high-stakes customer meeting, including quarterly business reviews:

☐ Seller prep for high-stakes customer meeting: Coordinates calendar invites with the customer and internal attendees. Aligns on an agenda with the customer. Works with the customer to create PowerPoint slides—the ownership of slide creation is with the seller, with the customer contributing.

☐ For high-stakes meetings with the customer, your seller will conduct the meeting as you and your seller planned and as agreed with the customer.

☐ For quarterly business reviews with the customer, the participants will discuss what is going well and what is not going well. The seller will review the customer's spend with your company. The customer will review their scorecard if they use one to track how you and your company are doing.

- ☐ Quarterly business reviews with the customer happen quarterly, as the name suggests. However, due to difficulty scheduling executive time on both sides, they may occur less frequently.
- ☐ Follow up: Your seller will write up and send out a recap of the meeting and agreed-upon actions to attendees.
- ☐ Your seller ensures the agreed-upon actions happen in the time frame expected.

ASSESSING IF IT WORKED

- ☐ Did your seller achieve the purpose of the customer meeting you and your seller discussed?
- ☐ Did the customer raise any surprises during the meeting?
- ☐ Did your seller get the business outcome they intended?
- ☐ Does your seller have a clear set of actions and next steps including scheduled follow-up meetings?
- ☐ Was the customer engaged?
- ☐ Did key customer executives attend the meeting?
- ☐ If this was a business review with the customer, did it go as planned?
- ☐ Did the customer raise concerns that need to be addressed?
- ☐ Was your seller prepared to speak to these concerns?
- ☐ Did your seller prioritize a set of actions to be taken over the next couple of months as a result of the meeting?

THINGS TO CONSIDER

It should be stated up front that I do not discuss every customer meeting my sellers have. I discuss only meetings where high-stakes outcomes exist or when there are formal connection points such as quarterly business reviews or executive meetings.

Listen and ask well-placed questions during the 1:1 meeting prep with your seller.

The types of questions I ask include: Who is attending? What are their expectations for the meeting?

If we have a deal we are working with the customer, we need to orchestrate who will ask for deal status and support from the senior customer executive attending the meeting.

If we are trying to expand our relationship within the account, my seller and I strategize in advance as to how we will ask for sponsorship and introductions to other parts of the customer organization.

If I am attending the customer meeting, I will typically take meeting notes and record follow-up actions. My purpose is to empower my seller to run and own the meeting.

Quarterly business reviews are an excellent way to get updated on the customer's business strategies and goals, as well as to understand what the customer is looking for from us and how we are performing. It's also a forum that fosters continued executive connection and relationship building.

CHAPTER 15

Preparing for Executive Meetings

Traditional Sales Managers...	As a Love Your Team Sales Manager, You...
Long for in-person customer meetings, dinners out, and golf games as a mechanism of building relationships. Build relationships directly with customers to mask their own lack of skill managing a team.	Give constructive feedback on executive briefing documents. Take notes for your sellers during executive meetings, leaving space for them to focus on conversation. Coach your sellers on executive engagement.

PURPOSE

To help your seller prepare for meetings between your executives and customer executives. There are two categories of executive meetings: executive sponsor meetings and topic-specific meetings with other executives. Conversations surrounding executive meetings have their own chapter because these meetings are strategically important and often complex. They take extra preparation and can take up to three months to arrange. Many enterprise accounts have at least one, if not two, executive sponsors on the seller's side—a business executive sponsor and a technical executive sponsor—who periodically meet with their customer counterparts. There are also peer-to-peer pairings, like CFO to CFO or chief HR officer to chief HR officer. Another example is an executive meeting to address specific customer challenges, usually involving relevant executives on both sides with domain expertise.

An executive sponsor meets regularly, at least quarterly, with their counterpart on the customer side. These are strategy discussions and checkpoints regarding critical projects both sides are jointly progressing. They are also opportunities to take a pulse on the health of the relationship. They are not a forum for escalations or immediate issues. Their purpose is to uncover persistent issues that need resolution at the organization level. These issues could be on either side. In contrast to quarterly business reviews, these are more private exchanges to chat about strategic topics and sensitive issues. If there is a hot issue, the executive with the domain expertise on the seller's side will conduct the meeting instead of the executive sponsor.

INTENDED OUTCOME

Build stronger relationships and value with the customer. Explore areas for strategic alignment and initiatives.

HOW TO RECOGNIZE THE NEED FOR THIS CONVERSATION

There's an upcoming executive meeting and preparation is needed.

HOW TO DO IT

There are two aspects to discuss here: the 1:1 meetings with the seller in preparation for the executive meeting and conducting the actual executive meeting.

1:1 meeting prep with your seller for executive meetings:

- ☐ Your seller sends out a meeting request for a 1:1 with you to prepare for an executive meeting.
- ☐ Seller prep: Your seller completes an executive briefing document outlining the intended outcome, issues, background of your business with the customer, and questions your seller would like your executive to ask. This document briefs your executive on the pertinent information for the upcoming executive meeting they will conduct.
- ☐ Conduct the 1:1 conversation: Your seller will review the briefing document with you in advance of them briefing your executive prior to the executive meeting with the customer. There may be iterations needed for the briefing document; either schedule additional meetings or use email to review the updated briefing document.
- ☐ If your executive requests a briefing meeting in advance of the customer meeting or you and your seller see the need for one, your seller will schedule and conduct a briefing for

the executive. You typically attend these meetings and may even take notes.

- ☐ Conducting the executive meeting with the customer:
- ☐ Your seller coordinates executive calendars and gets the executive meeting scheduled.
- ☐ Your seller will work with your executive's staff and the customer executive's staff to reach agreement on topics and agenda.
- ☐ Your seller participates in the executive meeting. They own the customer relationship and need to make sure they understand the issues discussed and follow-up needed.
- ☐ Your seller ghostwrites a thank-you email for your executive to send to the customer executive after the meeting.
- ☐ Follow up: Your seller communicates actions and ensures actions get done.

ASSESSING IF IT WORKED

- ☐ Did the meeting achieve its purpose?
- ☐ Were your executives engaged and prepared?
- ☐ Did the meeting help build a stronger relationship with the customer?

THINGS TO CONSIDER

I review the executive briefing documents created by my seller, making sure the topics are relevant and clearly defined and the content supports our goals for the meeting. Additionally, we specify what we want our executive to probe or address. Typically, I do not participate in the customer executive meeting. I play a critical behind-the-scenes role to ensure my seller has everything covered and our executive is well-prepared when meeting with the customer executive.

Executive meetings are an excellent way to build strong, durable relationships with customer executives. They provide an insider's insight as to what is really going on with the customer. They uncover opportunities for strategic partnerships and areas of the business where our solutions can add value. They are also time-consuming to execute.

Executive meetings are also an excellent way for sellers to be exposed to our executives. The visibility sellers get among our executive ranks can be an asset to a seller's career. It can also be career-limiting if a seller does not do an excellent job. It is high stakes all around.

CHAPTER 16

Resolving Customer Issues

Traditional Sales Managers...	As a Love Your Team Sales Manager, You...
Leave lots of broken glass in their wake from overselling. Leave it up to customer success, engineering, and "make it right" funds to improve customer satisfaction.	Listen. Seek to understand the customer's point of view. Ask clarifying questions to understand various viewpoints. Project an executive presence.

PURPOSE

To create customer satisfaction by helping your sellers navigate customer complaints and put plans in place to resolve them. In these conversations you coach your sellers to handle customer escalations. Despite your best intentions, customers will sometimes be dissatisfied. Major issues, such as a cloud service going down, impact the customer's ability to get their job done. Customers want these issues handled immediately. Other common issues range from delays in providing what a customer expects, to billing mistakes, to a seller not fitting well within the customer's culture. Some issues prompt immediate complaints and rapid escalation; some are minor inconveniences that fester and come out in satisfaction surveys. Either way, too much friction will get in the way of strong business relationships.

Establishing a trusting relationship with customers is important. Customers prefer someone with experience handling their issues, not someone new. They want someone who knows how to get things done.

A sales manager's knowledge of an issue often starts with a seller bringing that issue forward. This is typically followed by troubleshooting with the seller to figure out how best to solve the issue. For example, if a service goes down, your seller may orchestrate a customer confidence call.

Another way an issue may arise is that the customer makes you aware of it directly. For example, a seller may not be a good fit and the customer lets you know. In such a case you may provide additional coaching outlining behaviors the customer wants to see, or you may tell the seller to take a back seat while another seller on the team takes point.

INTENDED OUTCOME

The customer's issue is addressed to their satisfaction. If the issue cannot be addressed, the customer has accepted your proposal for a remedy or path forward to mitigate the concern. Customer satisfaction is sufficiently improved so they want to continue to do business with you and your company and your seller.

HOW TO RECOGNIZE THE NEED FOR THIS CONVERSATION

A customer raises concerns to you or your seller. This can happen in a few different ways. You might get poor customer satisfaction survey results. During regular executive syncs with the customer, they may inform you of an issue. Or an issue may come up in another meeting such as a quarterly business review or executive meeting.

HOW TO DO IT

- [ ] Have a 1:1 with your seller to review the customer's issue. This is typically a one-off meeting as you would not want to wait until your regularly scheduled meeting to discuss a hot issue.
- [ ] You and your seller establish a clear set of actions and internal resources that need to be mobilized to address the customer's issue.
- [ ] Your seller schedules a meeting with the customer to address their issue. This meeting will likely include experts from your side who are knowledgeable on the topic the customer raises, such as billing issues or service reliability.
- [ ] If the customer's issue is a concern about your seller, discuss the feedback with your seller and come up with a mitigation plan, which will likely include coaching your seller to change some of his or her behavior.

☐ Reach out to the customer directly to address and deescalate the customer's concern.

ASSESSING IF IT WORKED

☐ Are you and your seller clear on the action to take and the resources that are needed to address the customer's issue?

☐ Were you able to address the customer's issue?

☐ Do you and the customer have a clear set of actions?

☐ Do you have a cadence to checkpoint status until resolution?

THINGS TO CONSIDER

On my team, the buck stops with me. Therefore, it is important for me to build direct relationships with key customer executives, providing them a senior point of contact if they have an issue.

I may take the lead in customer issue resolution where the resolution is neither absolute nor within the time frame or scope that the customer prefers. This takes the heat off the seller and reduces their stress. Sometimes it is pragmatic and just makes sense for me to be the one to have the difficult conversation with the customer.

Some issues are easier to address than others. Some customer complaints may point to a systemic issue on our side that needs addressing.

Some complaints are a result of deliberate strategy decisions on our side because we are removing or adding resources to support the customer in ways that may not always delight them. Change is hard for everyone, our team and theirs.

It is important to keep the customer's business goals at the center of the conversation. This helps determine the impact and severity of the issues the customer raises and helps mobilize internal resources to address them.

SECTION 5

Conversations of Internal Alignment

Selling is a team sport. There are numerous sales leaders and sellers who must work collaboratively in order to effectively sell complex solutions to enterprise customers. It is common for different views to surface and these need to be discussed and agreed upon so that we can all show up coordinated and in alignment in front of the customer. In some cases, we need to agree to disagree and then commit to a plan of action going forward. As mentioned previously, in a large enterprise, it is not uncommon for 50 percent of a seller's time to be focused on ensuring internal team alignment and 50 percent of their time actually selling to the customer.

In this section I use the following terms frequently, so let's define them.

- Extended team—the individual contributors (specialized sellers, customer success, support, consulting, engineering, product management) who touch or support customers. They may be dedicated to your customer or come in and out of accounts.

- Key stakeholders—managers and leaders in your organization who have team members touching the customer or have a vested interest in your customer. They may serve as executive sponsors for your customers, for example.

It takes a village of great minds to make a deal in the innovation economy. The enterprise sale is complex. The customer is complex. The product is complex. It's orchestrating, not playing solo, and requires knowing just what to tweak to get everything moving in the right direction. It includes obtaining agreement and alignment with internal stakeholders, identifying and selling solutions that address customers' business challenges, and building relationships with decision makers who have the buying power to say yes.

For example, one of our competitors proposed their cloud service for a particular customer solution at a fraction of the normal industry price. The questions for internal alignment became: How do we meet that pricing request? Do we even want to? Our deal teams carry the keys to pricing decisions so my seller had to go through internal channels while at the same time responding to customer requests and time frames. The seller is not just orchestrating alignment within the customer's company; they are also orchestrating within their own company.

Sellers must have the skills to manage a large complex deal as a project. Everyone on the team from the CEO on down needs to understand the goal, the timeline, the customer's priorities, the decision process, and the decision criteria. During the course of a complex deal pursuit, it is not uncommon for the customer's decision criteria to change.

Each person on the extended team is assigned a role for which they maintain not only subject matter expertise but responsibility and authority. Your role as sales manager is not to lead the project but to ensure that all of this is done well and managed through to completion. It is your seller's responsibility to keep the internal team informed and on track throughout the sales pursuit to deal completion.

Consider a billion-dollar proposal. Or should I say, the fifth iteration of that proposal. The immediate sales team is ten people. Content specialists put the proposal together. Legal experts check the contract terms. Finance reviews pricing and discounts. Executives are apprised of additional considerations that might erode profit margin. And approvals must be sought at every step. The customer wants post-sale support, so support team members are brought in to help with this request. A third-party solution may also be part of the deal, and team members dedicated to that third-party relationship make sure your team works tightly with that partner to instill the customer's confidence that implementation will go smoothly.

All these human pieces must come together to define customer value and make a deal. And it's your account sellers who orchestrate it all, updating and keeping everyone on the same page so the deal doesn't get deadlocked by internal questions, concerns, and delays.

No one person knows everything to make a successful deal. Complex customers have complex requirements. One size doesn't fit all. You end up with specialists instead of generalists, people who know and can communicate a specific aspect of the solution.

Internal alignment is a reconciling of multiple viewpoints and concerns from different parts of your company that creates the opportunity for a solution that satisfies both your company and the customer. Your sellers know their customers, the product team knows the product, and the finance teams and company executives know the deal guardrails to maintain profitability and meet strategic goals. All must work together to get a deal done.

You can have a fantastic strategy that outlines what you need to do and which customer executives you need to convince that your solution meets their needs at a price point they can live with. However, if you do not get the internal stakeholders aligned to your strategy, the deal can get derailed, not by the customer saying no but by lack of support in your organization.

Time kills all deals—and nothing adds more time to a deal more than internal friction. In the complex world of enterprise selling, sometimes it can take up to eight weeks or longer to get internal alignment on a deal structure and pricing before the team can get a proposal to the customer. By that time, it may be too late. The customer either opts to move forward with a different solution or, very frequently, decides to do nothing. No decision is often the biggest competitor for enterprise sellers, so when a customer is ready to do a deal, agility and fast internal alignment are essential to making it happen.

We can boil all this down to a simple phrase: a seller sells to both sides.

Conversations of Internal Alignment coach your team through talking clearly with internal stakeholders about solutions, offers, and pricing—all of which increase sales and reduce sales cycles. As sales managers, we strategize with our sellers about ways to get internal alignment efficiently and effectively in order to structure deals that actually get done and meet customers' needs.

The three Conversations of Internal Alignment are:

1. Aligning the Extended Team—These discussions are focused on helping your seller get buy-in from extended team members on solution, strategy, and offering. The focus is on coaching your seller to take the action needed to ensure the extended team is coordinated and shows a united front to the customer. There may not be a specific deal at hand; instead it could be helping your seller work through a thorny customer issue that customer success is leading.

2. Securing Resources and Investments—These conversations center on helping your seller secure agreement and approval across internal stakeholders for a deal including investments, contract terms, discounts, and services.

3. Gaining Agreement on Partner Participation—These conversations determine the solution that you will propose to the customer. Will the solution include any third-party offerings from a partner? Or do you believe

you have all of the components of the solution "in-house" and can meet your customer's needs by offering only your own products and services?

CHAPTER 17

Aligning the Extended Team

Traditional Sales Managers...	As a Love Your Team Sales Manager, You...
Have a team in name only. Do not spend time coaching their teams. Focus only on what the seller does, instead of collaborating across the company. Focus on customers and underestimate the internal selling needed to deliver results.	Spend time with your sellers coaching and strategizing. Understand that using all of the internal resources available is the fastest way toward achieving revenue goals. Build strong relationships with internal leaders who support or touch your customer: product sales, customer success, finance, product management, and customer executive sponsors.

(Table continued)

Traditional Sales Managers...	As a Love Your Team Sales Manager, You...
	Collaborate with colleagues and internal leaders to brainstorm strategies and seek their insights to inform decision-making.
	Demonstrate strong communication, leadership, and influence skills.
	Value building a strong internal network.
	Recognize that a seller's job includes internal selling.

PURPOSE

To help sellers get internal alignment across their extended team. Leading an extended team is no small thing. There are usually interpersonal relationship issues. Some extended team members may not take actions expected of their role. There are often disagreements across the extended team on how to approach a deal. And while it is ideal for individual contributors to work out an approach without getting management involved, the seller leading the extended team must always be involved.

Securing this internal alignment and leading their extended team is the seller's job.

Enterprise sellers are expected to lead a cross-functional team of specialist sellers, customer success, and support resources that do not report directly to them. This can be complex as there are often fifty people who touch an account regularly and another thirty who get involved with that customer from time to time. Divisive views undermine team cohesion and the sales pursuit strategy. Roles and responsibilities need to be clearly understood and agreed upon.

Conversations surrounding extended team alignment provide the seller with clarity on how to remove sales blockers quickly and solve thorny customer issues even when there is a diversity of opinion on how to address them. These conversations enable the seller to get support from internal stakeholders, horizontally and vertically, on account and deal strategy and solving customer issues. It is important that these conversations only include those stakeholders who are necessary to solve the issue at hand.

One goal of extended team alignment is to keep deals on track and make sure resources are used effectively and efficiently. This need is ongoing throughout a sales cycle, not a one-and-done thing. Deals are complex, with lots of moving parts and people, and there are always new deal quirks and asks that need alignment across the team.

Here are two examples of situations I've experienced where internal alignment conversations were required:

- One of my sellers was frustrated because a customer implementation was not going as planned. The customer success manager was also frustrated. The situation was that the customer needed to buy additional services from us in order to realize the value they required from the solution they purchased. Customer success required sales to reengage. It is not uncommon for additional requirements like these to be added after a sale. There was some finger-pointing going on as to what the customer actually required and who from our side would provide it. This situation precipitated a call that included managers from customer success, sales, and engineering, who had a part to play due to their long-term relationship with this early-adopter customer. No one part of our organization could solve this issue on their own. My seller got us all on a call and we discussed the situation in depth and formulated a plan of action that resulted in a successful implementation.

- I had a situation where a product specialist seller believed we should insist the customer provide dedicated resources to implement our solution. Others on the account team disagreed and thought the resources should come from our own team. This disagreement on our stance with the customer was creating friction across our team that was impossible for my seller to sort out independently. Emotions ran high. I set up a call with my peer managers to discuss and sort out our strategy. We came to an agreement on a path forward that satisfied the customer and our internal team.

INTENDED OUTCOME

Your seller has clarity on how to align the extended team to solve the situation they are concerned about. Your seller is able to gain sufficient agreement across internal stakeholders to lead the extended team as they move forward with clear next steps and actions.

HOW TO RECOGNIZE THE NEED FOR THIS CONVERSATION

A seller brings up a situation involving their extended team, or you learn about an issue from an extended team member or manager.

When there is a clear disconnect among team members supporting the account on how to solve customer issues, it becomes vital to have an alignment conversation. Extended team issues can take many forms, including how to respond to a complex or unusual customer request, what solution to offer, internal head count and resources needed to support a customer, and renegotiating a customer agreement set to expire. The goal of extended team alignment is twofold: first to show a united front when interacting and meeting with a customer or presenting to senior internal leadership, and second to solve a customer issue or secure resources required to strengthen a customer relationship and move a deal forward if there is one at hand.

HOW TO DO IT

☐ You and your seller discuss the issue. Ask questions to understand what is really going on. Discuss pros and cons of different approaches. Continue discussing the issue until your seller has clarity on how to move forward.

☐ The most likely next step from this discussion with your seller is one of the following:

  ☐ Your seller is confident they can solve the issue on their own by meeting directly with the extended team members or stakeholders to sort out the disconnects and gain alignment.

  ☐ You and your seller agree that management support is needed to get alignment across the extended team. What is needed is a stakeholder alignment meeting. A stakeholder alignment meeting is a meeting where all of the people who have a vested interest in the topic being discussed come together to share their views with the objective of finding a path forward that all can agree on. You will probably want to do a dry run with your seller in advance of the alignment meeting.

  ☐ Send this meeting invite to the extended team members, their managers, and other key stakeholders. This meeting could be in a conference room, remote, or hybrid. Send this meeting invite out from your calendar so other managers prioritize and attend.

  ☐ Your seller conducts the alignment meeting. You participate to help support the conversation.

  ☐ Follow up: Make sure there is a clear action plan and next steps as a result of the alignment meeting. Your seller sends out notes from the discussion and next steps agreed upon during the meeting.

ASSESSING IF IT WORKED

- ☐ Does your seller have clarity on the action needed to address the situation raised?
- ☐ Did everyone understand the issue being discussed and work together to address it?
- ☐ Is there agreement across your seller's extended team and key stakeholders on how to proceed?
- ☐ Did everyone have an opportunity to speak up and were all views heard?

THINGS TO CONSIDER

I've observed that a typical enterprise seller spends 45–50 percent of their time selling their ideas within their own company. It's not a trivial business. A big part of this job is aligning the extended team.

Getting alignment can be tough when there are diverse and passionate opinions. I have found it important to build strong relationships with key stakeholders in the organization in advance of having what may end up being a difficult discussion.

CHAPTER 18

Securing Resources and Investments

Traditional Sales Managers...	As a Love Your Team Sales Manager, You...
Push and alienate the deal review team to approve discounts without understanding the discount and decision process.	Know how to build a case for discounting, other investments, and resources. Empower and coach your sellers to pitch the business case supporting the investments needed to win a deal, including requested discounts, to the deal review board.

PURPOSE

To secure the investments necessary to win deals. Examples of investments are discounts, contract terms, and non-monetary resources such as implementation services.

It is typical that large customers will not pay list price for what they buy. A phase of the sales cycle inevitably includes negotiating price, contract terms, and non-product investments needed to help the customer be successful. This is such an important phase of the sales cycle that I've devoted this chapter to it. Many companies have a very structured approach for requesting discounts, investments, changes to contractual terms, or any other resources to support a deal. As a sales manager, it is critical you understand these approaches and processes and coach your sellers to work effectively within your company's structure.

In addition to the formal process for seeking investments, it is important, if not required, to get alignment across internal stakeholders before making a formal investment request. There are many ways to structure a deal and each has short- and long-term implications. At a minimum, your seller will need to get support and agreement on pricing, investment, and discounting from your immediate management chain. Once there is alignment on deal approach, your seller is ready to take the business case forward to justify the investment asks they are making.

Internal alignment is not just with the sales team. It includes product teams, finance teams, industry teams, strategic pursuit teams, executives—all the resources internal to an organization to help respond to proposals, write technical responses, move deal pursuits forward, solve customer challenges, and take care of the other trappings of a deal.

Some internal alignment conversations focus around a specific deal. Some help solve post sales issues, such as implementation challenges or joint business venture complications.

INTENDED OUTCOME

Efficiently and quickly get needed investments, discounts, contract terms, and other resources in a time frame the customer accepts. Gain clarity on your company's appetite to invest and win the deal. Win the deal and generate incremental revenue.

HOW TO RECOGNIZE THE NEED FOR THIS CONVERSATION

Your seller informs you that a deal will not move forward unless the customer gets a better price, contractual terms, or investments. Of course, if your seller can sell your solution at list price with standard terms and no investments, they should do that!

HOW TO DO IT

There are two aspects to discuss here: the 1:1 meetings with your seller in preparation for the deal review board meeting and conducting the actual deal review board meeting.

1:1 meeting prep with your seller for deal review board meeting:

- ☐ Your seller reviews with you their deal structure and proposal including discount, contract terms, and investment requests. You provide feedback and iterate with your seller until they gain your approval.
- ☐ Once your seller has your approval, you and your seller gain approval from your management chain.

Presenting to the deal review board:

- ☐ Your seller requests a deal review and the meeting is scheduled.
- ☐ Your seller presents the business case and asks for approval. During the meeting, you may want to take notes in the background with particular attention to feedback from the deal review board and resulting action items. This allows your seller to focus on the conversation, including presenting the case, answering questions, and discussing next steps.

ASSESSING IF IT WORKED

- ☐ Was your seller able to get approval for requested price discounts, contractual terms, and other investments they can take back to the customer to negotiate a strong deal?
- ☐ Did your seller get clarity on your company's appetite to win this deal?
- ☐ Can your seller restructure the business case or deal to get an approval they can use to continue negotiating with their customer?

THINGS TO CONSIDER

Once the investments, discounts, and contract terms are approved by the deal review board, it is critical that your proposal back to the customer is packaged carefully. Anticipate further asks. It is usually smart to not present all of the investments that have been approved so your seller has room to negotiate and avoid going back to the deal review board.

Of course during the proposal iterations, there will be conversations with the extended team. I coach my sellers to make the distinction between input from those who have the power to say yes or no and those who are simply expressing their opinion.

CHAPTER 19

Gaining Agreement on Partner Participation

Traditional Sales Managers...	As a Love Your Team Sales Manager, You...
Use maximizing revenue attainment as the sole criterion when deciding whether or not to work with a partner on a deal. Look at revenue and partnering with a short-term time horizon.	Understand that partners are sometimes essential to your business. Understand how you can scale your business by working with partners. Understand partners' offerings and value-add and coach your seller to develop strong partner relationships. Ensure channel managers are part of your seller's extended team for deal pursuits to provide guidance on how and when to bring a partner into the deal.

PURPOSE

To ensure that broad criteria are considered when deciding the role a partner might play in a sales pursuit.

In complex enterprise sales, partners offer a wide range of services that manufacturers cannot provide. These include managing risk, integration services, providing missing product features, and processing transactions, to name a few. Because partners might be considered critical to your overall business, there may be pressure to include partner solutions as a component of every proposal. While the extended team will provide input, your seller must decide if it is better to work with a partner, or multiple partners, to expand and enhance your solution offering to meet the customer's requirement. There are sometimes internal disagreements on how to move forward. In my experience, the seller with coaching from their immediate manager must make the final decision.

It is important that the customer's goals and requirements are the focus of every conversation. You may need to remind stakeholders to put their own metrics aside and objectively consider what is in the best interest of the customer and your company.

INTENDED OUTCOME

To ensure partners are objectively considered and included in customer proposals.

HOW TO RECOGNIZE THE NEED FOR THIS CONVERSATION

There's a lack of agreement on the "right"' solution for the customer. Typical considerations for whether or not to include a partner are:

- Will the partner enhance the overall solution and value for the customer?
- Can you meet the customer's requirements with your first-party offering?
- Will including a partner increase your ability to win the deal?
- Will the partner help you scale your business?

HOW TO DO IT

☐ Your seller sends a meeting invite to key internal stakeholders to discuss the partner strategy for a deal. This meeting must have your support and involvement. Such discussions are often difficult and sometimes heated and your skills and experience may be needed to keep the discussion objective.

☐ During the conversation, your seller:

1. Outlines the customer's buying criteria and business requirements.

2. Outlines the solution, its gaps, and partner offerings that can add value to close those gaps.

3. Leads an objective discussion with stakeholders with the goal of getting alignment and reaching the best decision.

☐ Follow up: After the meeting, debrief with your seller and help them make a decision on how to move forward.

ASSESSING IF IT WORKED

☐ Did a discussion take place objectively reviewing the pros and cons of including a partner in the solution proposal?

□ Were all participants' views heard and considered?

□ Was a decision made, even if there was not agreement across all stakeholders?

THINGS TO CONSIDER

It is impossible to be current on all offerings from all partners. It is the job of your seller to have a solid understanding of key partners that are relevant to their customers. I expect my team to share information that helps all of the team work more effectively with partners. I also set up calls with partners regularly to understand their offerings and, where appropriate, connect them with my sellers to explore areas of collaboration.

PART III

UNIVERSAL CONVERSATIONAL COMPETENCIES

CHAPTER 20

Conversational Skills

Universal conversational competencies include overarching skills that apply to every conversation outlined in this book. Acquiring and strengthening these skills helps a sales manager be more effective when coaching a sales team and interacting through various modes of communication, including face-to-face, audio and video calls, and written. While the skills discussed below may add value more broadly to conversational effectiveness in other contexts—and feel free to use them as such—I am not a conversational specialist by trade, and therefore I only speak to the skills needed for sales managers.

Skilled conversations nurture strong teams, support seller performance, and ultimately reduce regrettable attrition. These skills are essential to your effective performance as a sales manager. A poorly executed conversation is often worse than no conversation at all. The conversational skills you model with your sellers will carry over to their conversations with customers fostering strong trust relationships and clarity around goals, process, and business value.

For efficiency's sake, I've arranged these skills in alphabetical order.

ASSUME POSITIVE INTENT

Assuming positive intent means maintaining the position that we all are on the same team, sincerely working toward common goals. This skill is the starting point for navigating every tough conversation. Before any tough conversation, I take a moment to remind myself to assume positive intent. It is impossible to listen for understanding unless you first assume positive intent. It is way too easy to blame.

Tough conversations happen. People are fallible. We fall into power plays, have personal biases, and make mistakes. When sellers, extended team members, and other stakeholders don't agree with each other, assuming positive intent creates space to move toward understanding within a respectful dialogue. By assuming good intent, it is much easier to identify areas of difference, find opportunities for alignment, and craft a path forward together.

In one of my recent meetings discussing a late-stage iteration of a complex deal, a fellow manager abruptly asked, "Wait a minute, why are we doing more discounts?" I easily could have taken it as a cheap shot. Instead I took a moment to remind myself to assume positive intent. The outburst could have been read as a rude challenge to my authority, and I could have responded defensively or even angrily at being interrupted. But I didn't. Assuming good intent, I responded as if my colleague legitimately did not know what I was talking about. I reexplained, patiently, calmly, and without condescension, "No, we're not doing more discounts. We're repackaging our offering in this proposal. And the reason is to create clarity of value and to provide additional context for the customer." The colleague settled down and brought up no further questions. What could have been a tense situation leading to an increase of confusion or challenging behavior instead was defused quickly and the meeting proceeded.

CADENCE

As a manager, you must rigorously manage your time. Failure to manage your time efficiently and effectively puts a burden on your team. Each team member is relying on you to be available to them when issues they can't solve on their own arise. They depend on you to have the right conversations at the right times so they have the support they need to focus on selling.

Of course, you weren't put in a sales management role unless you already had solid time management skills. But the Love Your Team system requires an additional skill: fitting all the needed conversations into the total time you have available. Between your reporting responsibilities, customer meetings, internal meetings, handling time-critical demands from your boss, and occasional firefighting, prioritizing conversations with your team might seem overwhelming.

The key is to design, set up, and execute a regular cadence of meetings with each member of your team, and the most important meeting is the regularly scheduled 1:1. Your 1:1 cadence, like everything else in this system, is not identical for each of your sellers.

Initially, you and each seller need to establish a 1:1 cadence that works for both of you. Most importantly, each 1:1 cadence needs to fit into that seller's professional and life rhythms. In the true spirit of servant leadership, you may find yourself with a 1:1 cadence with a seller in a remote time zone that obliges you to wake up and be ready to have effective conversations at an inconvenient hour. My advice is to absorb the inconvenience in exchange for the obvious positive impact of showing, repeatedly, you care about your seller's life sufficiently to adapt to them.

Over time, you may find it necessary to change the 1:1 cadence for a specific seller, usually in response to the need for more conversations about performance or a critical deal that requires more frequent 1:1s to stay on track and keep you informed. It is important to make this adjustment quickly when performance issues arise. These conversations are at the heart of performance management. Because of this, it's a good idea to look ahead to this possibility as you set up your calendar. For example, if your initial 1:1 cadence with a given seller is to meet on the first and third Thursday of each month at 4:00 p.m. local time for them, it is smart to block the same time on the second and fourth Thursday each month for work you need to do, such as inspecting your pipeline, checking that your CRM is up to date, or preparing for the next forecast meeting. That way, if you decide that particular seller has a need for more frequent 1:1 meetings to have performance conversations, you won't need to change the 1:1 cadence with other team members. The burden of adapting to find time for your individual work then falls where it should as a Love Your Team leader: on you. I always let my sellers know that we will make adjustments to our regular 1:1 schedule as needed. Critical customer meetings sometimes fall on scheduled 1:1s. In that case, we find another time slot in the same week for that 1:1.

It's very important to note that your 1:1 cadence with each member of your team is not a cadence of prespecified conversations. You and your seller will come to each meeting with an agenda that includes the conversations needed at that specific meeting. Some 1:1s will have only one conversation type, but others may have three or four or more. It depends on what you decide is needed to make sure that specific seller is getting the support and resources they need to do their job while living their life. In this way, your 1:1s are naturally varied, impactful, and valued by each team member, rather than settling into the "same old, same old" rut that is way too common in old-school sales management.

Here's how I use meeting cadences to make sure I provide my team with the conversations they need.

Until very recently, I managed a twelve-person strategic enterprise sales team. Every other week, I held thirty-minute 1:1 meetings with ten of them. I held weekly 1:1s with the other two sellers—in one case because the person asked for the more frequent cadence, and in the other case because I asked for it out of concern for that team member's performance.

In addition, I also held forty-five-minute formal performance checkpoint meetings three times per year with each team member. These checkpoint meeting sets were each concentrated in a two-week period. And finally, every two weeks, I held forty-five-minute pipeline review meetings with each of my five account teams. Our reporting and CRM tools allowed me to know the numbers, but I didn't know the color commentary or context. For example, why didn't that customer want to move forward? What was the next action needed to move the deal forward? You can't create a plan to remove deal blockers unless you have these conversations.

To save you doing the math, I laid out and executed meeting cadences that totaled 306.5 hours per year, or an average of 25.5 hours per month. Even if I were to work only forty hours per week, these meetings only directly took up 15 percent of my total work-week. Throw in one hour of prep time for each hour of meeting and my cadence of meetings with my team occupied 30 percent of my work time, leaving plenty of time for the many other things I chose to do for my own professional development and personal well-being: building relationships both inside and outside Micro-soft, seeking advice, getting needed training, handling my report-ing duties—and taking care of the myriad things in my personal life that don't fit neatly outside of standard work hours.

To be very clear, the purpose of having a set cadence for 1:1s and team meetings is to provide a framework within which you will deploy many different types of conversations. The art of managing the Love Your Team way is in recognizing which conversations are best for each meeting, how much time is optimal to invest in each conversation type on each meeting agenda, and, of course, your skill in holding each of those conversations. As a manager, you must prepare for each of the conversations you have chosen for each meeting and then bring your whole self to each of those conversations, taking care to keep in mind both the purpose of that specific conversation and the conversational skills you know you need to execute that type of conversation effectively and gracefully.

I also do out-of-cycle 1:1s if needed. Don't wait. Ten members of my team were located in different parts of the United States, but one team member was in India and another was in Israel. Remote means even more attention to these conversations, not less. There's no office hallway or lunchroom passings for quick "How are you doing?" check-ins, so the only way to build connection is through scheduled calls.

This bouquet of checkpoints makes for a lot of meetings. Be on top of things. Keep a detailed calendar, even down to when you're expecting a follow-up or response to a conversation. This helps with staying organized and ensuring details don't fall through the cracks. Dropping the ball or missing a checkpoint may not seem like a big deal, but it's these little things that can erode team trust and engagement over time.

CHEERLEADING

It's easy to get bogged down in negative inertia because of all the noes, both internally and externally, that are part of every seller's experience. As the person who sees the big picture, part of your job as sales manager is to motivate and focus your team by framing setbacks in a positive light, as opportunities for the future, and as normal steps toward accomplishing a greater purpose.

This isn't a Pollyanna style of cheerleading. I'm not saying make light of everything or leave real roadblocks unacknowledged when things get complicated or go off the rails. Good managers cheerlead *through* those obstacles, not around them. Encouragement is an act of reframing. If we can't do this, what can we do? There is a lot of change that happens within the company and with our customers. Providing context and the why behind change enables your team to be at ease and focus on selling.

Positive motivation isn't sustained by rewards, bell-ringing, rah-rah, or pats on the back. To keep people energized, help them keep perspective. They don't have to stay in the hole they're in; there are ways out. As manager, you are in the best position to give that team member the resources and knowledge to get out of that hole. Conversely, by ignoring a struggling team member, you are allowing that hole to get deeper, potentially impacting their attitude and performance well beyond their current challenges.

As an example, a seller is trying to figure out a way for us to provide an acceptable solution to a customer. There are a lot of demands and a lot of "not good enoughs." It's easy for your seller to get discouraged. As manager, my job is to step in and put the situation in perspective, perhaps even reassuring the seller we don't have to pursue the deal if the company doesn't want this business. There are *always* more deals to be done.

And it's not just encouraging team members through problems. It's coaching them on being better cheerleaders for themselves, their customers, and their own teams so they don't always have to rely on you to maintain optimism.

Cheerleading is one of the conversational competencies that's essential for your team to adopt. What can they consciously do when they find themselves sinking into a negative rut? How can they reframe? To help team members practice cheerleading, use moments of negativity as a chance for the team member to work on their personal development, maybe by cultivating an approach that is more flexible and less controlling.

CLARIFICATION

As a manager, you must always clarify the situation at hand, unpacking any potential confusion. Clarification starts with the words used in the communication, then digs into the real intent or need behind those words, eventually reaching mutual understanding. The clarification is most often to provide context. It may also be to provide understanding of differing viewpoints.

Out of necessity, enterprise companies use acronyms and language unique to that organization. A sales leader may talk about a specific sales strategy and give it a unique name. Nobody outside your organization would know what that unique name is referencing. Some companies create glossaries that define common acronyms, terms, and programs. In many cases it becomes necessary for you to clarify what is meant when those common terms and names are confusing to your team. This is especially necessary with new team members, who often silently struggle with understanding your company's private language, making them feel less included and therefore unable to fully participate in the conversation. In short, don't assume. Clarify.

Another common situation is when inevitably colleagues or people on your team will use a "word salad" to convey a concept. They use a lot of words but really do not say anything that makes sense. By asking for clarification rather than faking understanding you don't have, you will help everyone on the team be clearer in their own communication.

The next area is to clarify technical, situational, and policy context for any actions you are asking of your team. This level of clarification is essential to support effective execution and foster accountability. In your explanation of context, include specific results, outcomes, time frames, and deadlines and why the action matters. Include the form any follow-up or action will take (e.g., an email updating you on the outcome of a deal conversation, an update to the pipeline by a specific date, or providing a slide you need for an internal presentation). Don't ask your sellers to read your mind.

Finally, it's important to clarify viewpoints to avoid and address misunderstandings. Sales always involves helping others move from their current point of view and level of understanding to a new point of view that supports change. As managers, we must bring the skill of clarification to every conversation to make sure that both parties' points of view are clear and understood. Otherwise, we have no starting point for considering the possibility of change, whether that change is within a deal, focused on performance improvement, or concerned with team culture.

COACHING

It is rare that a conversation doesn't offer an opportunity for coaching. At the very least, a coaching mindset is a good starting point whenever you are having a conversation with one of your sellers.

The key to the conversational skill of coaching is to ask questions so that your seller discovers the answer to their challenge. This requires that you stay curious and avoid giving advice as long as possible. I learned this technique of coaching by going through a course called "The Coaching Habit" led by Michael Bungay Steiner. His company is called boxofcrayons.com. Check it out.

Curiosity keeps you listening and helps you ask follow-on questions. These questions help your seller isolate the real issue and provide you clarity on what's really going on. It is nearly impossible to understand what your seller really needs if you jump into advice giving. Your advice is likely to miss the mark, unless you've asked enough questions to understand the situation. Refrain from jumping in to fix problems. It's likely you'll end up fixing the wrong thing. In any conversation, it can be tempting to take charge and offer a solution as soon as you believe you understand the challenge your seller is facing. By staying curious and asking more questions, you uncover what is on your seller's mind, how they see their situations and challenges, and courses of action they have considered.

As a sales manager, you Love Your Team best when your coaching conversational skill is "always on" rather than being reserved for a special coaching session. The more you apply this skill, the more effective every conversation that is part of the Love Your Team system will be.

COMMUNICATION

Communication is more than telling someone your thoughts. It includes the methods and media by which we convey information. And the little things speak volumes.

It's important to be clear with your team about your communication preferences, both when you first start working with them and along the way as you discover communication challenges. Let your team know, with clarity, when and how you like to receive messages, and be specific about your meaning of "timely fashion" and expectations for follow-ups.

Many communication challenges revolve around the most ubiquitous medium in business: email. Email does not equal communication. Sending an email doesn't mean the recipient reads, understands, and acts upon it. Nor does it mean that the recipient will correctly interpret your intent. When reading email, your team members can easily misread directness for criticism, or even the fact that you copied another team member or a peer of yours as undermining. This is a topic I frequently return to with my team. They often forget that email does not equal communication and cannot figure out why the person on the receiving end of the email did not take action.

When you really need conversational clarity, pick up the phone and schedule a meeting. A true back-and-forth conversation is the best way to check comprehension and accountability.

When another manager took a product seller off one of my team's accounts, I didn't just send an email. I instant messaged my colleague to see if they were available for a quick conversation. I talked to that manager. I talked to the team member who was taken off. I talked to my own seller. All to diagnose accurately what had happened and why and to determine what next steps would be.

Holding multiple conversations may sound like it would take longer, but it takes less time to schedule and have a conversation than to compose a long email that doesn't get read and delays critical problem-solving. For speed of action, there's no substitute for conversation.

The amount of information that can be communicated in a conversation is exponentially more than in written communication on its own. There are ten bits of information in one letter or character. The average email only has about 5,000 bits of information in it. If you're communicating something that's complex and involves emotion and decision-making, it takes more than 5,000 bits. And you don't even know if the recipient read and absorbed all those bits. The human voice carries about 20,000 bits of information per second, which translates to four emails of information in that second. It's all emotional communication done with tone of voice, pace, cadence—the things we feel when someone speaks to us. So if you're trying to collaborate on complex deals, a ten-second conversation will do the work of forty emails. And you'll know the other person heard you.

CONSTRUCTIVE FEEDBACK

Constructive feedback is feedback that seeks to help a person improve and develop skills. It is not helpful to use subjective terms like "bad" or "good." I provide constructive feedback after an important customer meeting or internal executive deal review when I've had the opportunity to see the seller in action. We will often debrief, and they want to know what I think. I start by asking them what they believe went well and was effective and what could have gone better. I provide my perspective. We discuss next steps and actions for the seller to take.

There are times when I receive feedback from other managers or extended team members that one of my sellers is not being effective in a specific area of their role. I will ask others who may have observed what happened leading to the assessment of my seller not being effective. Once I've gathered all of the information I can, I will have a conversation with my seller about the assessment that they are not as effective as needed in a domain of their role. I will ask the seller for their thoughts on the situation. It is super important to listen carefully. Just having this conversation is likely to trigger defensiveness or anxiety. I am seeking to understand what's going on, not to accuse. Ideally, we will have a constructive conversation about the situation and both of us will come away with a clearer understanding; likely both of us will have actions to take.

There are times when these feedback conversations get very emotional, and the seller gets very defensive. Despite my attempts to defuse the emotion, I cannot. I will suggest that we meet again in a day or two to discuss further. When we meet again, both of us have had time to think and we can often have a more rational discussion on the situation and feedback at hand.

It is important to be as clear and specific as you can when giving feedback. This can be tricky as your seller will be tempted to ask, "Who told you that?" For the sake of confidentiality, you cannot say. What's important is to focus on the observed actions and how they differ from the expected behavior of your seller.

CONTEXT

I sometimes feel that the main responsibility of the sales manager is to provide context and seek context. Context is the background information that informs what is happening in the foreground. Below are common areas of conversation where understanding context is critical.

Your Team Members

What situation is happening in the life of a team member that may explain their behavior at work? Is a family member sick? Did the nanny not show up for work? Has there been a death in the family? All of this impacts your team member's ability to focus on work and be effective. If a team member's results or behavior suddenly changes, it is a signal to check in and find out what is going on. It may be that your seller needs extra leeway for the day or week. You will need to adjust and perhaps fill in on a meeting they were scheduled to conduct.

During the pandemic lockdowns, one of my team members had to both work from home and homeschool his children. Everyone in the household competed for network bandwidth. He helped with schoolwork and made sure it got done. He was simultaneously an employee, parent, and teacher in a household space that did triple duty as workspace, living space, and classroom. I could not expect him to have the same work capacity and focus as he had pre-pandemic. The pandemic taught us to have more grace and understanding for our team members, colleagues, and customers. Everyone was going through something, even if we did not always know exactly what.

Bear in mind the working environment and responsibilities of team members may require adjusting expectations and workload based on what the team member is able to do. These adjustments allow work to get done while minimizing disruption. It also lets my team know I have their back, increasing their trust and loyalty.

Deals in the Pipeline

The majority of time in a pipeline review is spent asking about the background context of a deal. What are the issues? Has the decision maker changed? Do we have deal sponsorship, and if not, what actions need to happen to get sponsorship? All of these questions are designed to understand the context of the situation so the right set of actions can be taken to progress the deal.

Organizational Change

Change is a constant and it is imperative that you as the manager provide your team with context, the why behind the changes your team is experiencing. These changes may be interpreted as positive; for example, the company decided to invest more resources in your business. Who in the company did this? What is the perceived opportunity the company wants to capture with these additional resources? The changes may be interpreted by your team as negative; for example, the company is moving your sales team and you into a newly formed organization. Why is the company making this change? What do they want to accomplish? Who are the new leaders? Will your team still have a job? When these changes occur, often at the start of a new fiscal year, you must spend more time communicating with your team. Change can create anxiety and your goal is to create stability, calm, and perspective in a moment of destabilization.

CONVERSATIONAL TONES

Tone speaks to the emotion or attitude that flavors the actual words of a conversation. The speaker can project curiosity, empathy, playfulness, or humor. How you approach a conversation with tone of voice, language choice, and body language can make a difference in how the other person responds. Having predictable and consistent tone creates trust. Especially when having difficult performance management conversations, being even-toned, compassionate, and clear will make all the difference in having a constructive outcome. Think through your tone and what you want to convey. What tone works best for this particular seller in this situation?

It used to be acceptable in a business context to yell and demonstrate superiority over others. Sales managers were known for getting angry with their team if the results did not come in or a seller missed their forecast. This doesn't cut it, as if it ever did. Adopting a constructive tone can be learned. The best way to do this is to be a person who is genuinely curious, empathetic, and interested in what the other person has to say. Act as if the other person is your peer or your customer rather than your subordinate and see what that does to change your tone.

Take stock of your own emotions. If you feel angry, chances are you're going to sound angry. That is likely to create anxiety, fear, defensiveness, and anger in others. Monitor your own physical reactions. Is your heart rate up? Are you breathing faster? Do you feel flushed or tense? If so, take a step back. Postpone the conversation until you've calmed down.

Some tips for handling emotion in the moment:

- Take a pause. Wait until tomorrow if you have to, until the emotion passes and you regain neutrality and perspective. Don't hesitate to be transparent in these moments: "I'm getting a little frustrated and need to take a step back." These admissions also give your team members permission to check and admit their emotions too.
- Write it down, reflect, revise. If you're sending an email responding to a heated topic, write out what you want to say and save the draft. Sleep on it. Review and revise in the morning. Maybe don't send it at all. Reach out and have a conversation instead.

On the other side of the tonal spectrum are soft-spoken, almost lazy tones. These tones are not necessarily a bad thing. You have to be willing to be authentic and truthful and engage in a way that is meaningful. Traditionally, soft-spokenness has often been attributed to weakness or submissiveness. The role of sales manager requires a level of strength and fortitude above the norm. There are many people who speak softly but carry a big stick, as Teddy Roosevelt famously said.

Strength and leadership does not equal aggression; it equals assertion. It equals the ability to know when a team member requires a bit of force and hardness, and when they require a lighter touch and just slight redirection. Soft tones also serve to deescalate situations. It's hard to keep yelling when the other person is not.

Constructive feedback and performance management tones: curious, matter-of-fact, and clear. Say what needs to be said in a straightforward, clear tone bordering on being firm.

Problem-solving meeting tone: clear, objective, curious, strong, assertive. Seek to understand and then drive actions and decisions.

IDEATION

Ideation is focused on coming up with new ideas beyond the boundaries of what an individual can do alone. Specifically for managers, it is about problem-solving with your seller. It includes asking questions and brainstorming actions to take. Example actions may be speaking with people or scheduling meetings—in short, coming up with ideas to unblock something that is stalled, often a deal.

Ideation involves one or more people by definition. It is important for sales managers to be adept at facilitating these brainstorming sessions. There are two core elements:

Asking good questions—For example, your seller is trying to build relationships with more customer executives. What are they trying to accomplish by having a relationship with a customer executive? Which customer executives are they targeting? Why do we need it? Is the executive scheduled to deliver a keynote address at an industry conference we are also attending?

Brainstorming actions to take—Look at LinkedIn to see if we know someone at our company who knows the executive. Ask a friendly customer executive to introduce us to the executive we are trying to meet. Have an executive on our side reach out to the executive we want to meet. Meet the target executive at a conference where he or she is scheduled to deliver a keynote address. As a manager, you want to understand the situation and help your team member problem-solve. It is important to think through how this might play out and what actions are needed to move forward and become actionable.

KNOWLEDGE

Sales managers get hired into a sales management role for a myriad of reasons. Typically there is knowledge they possess or expertise they have that they can build upon to be successful in the role. However, I've never met a sales manager who is knowledgeable in all areas critical to the role they are stepping into. Who would want a job like that, where they already know everything and there is nothing new to learn? Not me!

Sales managers, like sellers, need to be always learning. The types of knowledge sales managers need include domain, operational, product, content, networking, culture building, leadership, industry, and how to get things done at your company.

Having this knowledge is good, but knowing when and how to offer it to your sellers as a resource is the real skill.

PURPOSE AND MEANING

The question "Why are we doing this?" establishes a connection to purpose and meaning. We create our own stories about why this career or job matters to us. This is the meaning we ascribe to the stories we create. Purpose can be achieving the bigger business outcomes and goals of the organization, such as increasing stock price and company value, or something more personal, like job benefits or success in the eyes of your community or spouse. Sometimes those purposes dovetail, such as when part of an employee's benefits includes company stock, making increasing that price a personal investment for the employee.

More likely than not, the purpose your sellers have for the work they do for you and the company has nothing to do with the company or you. You are a means to an end and they are working for their own purposes and the meaning they create in their own story about why they do this job. This job, and most likely your company, is just a stop along the way on their career journey. It is likely they are doing the job to save for a home, take care of their family, be financially independent, and retire early. Have you heard of the FIRE (financially independent, retire early) movement?

Meaning has become much more important in a post-pandemic world. The why behind the work and company matters. Do the company's values align? Are the executives walking the talk? Does the company have initiatives around issues that matter to me, such as social justice, immigration law, sustainability? Your sellers can work for anybody and any company. A differentiator in job decision criteria is now purpose and meaning along with flexibility and adequate pay and benefits.

You may be thinking, *I cannot influence this. These are the company's values and initiatives, not mine.* There is some truth to that, to be sure. Think about what matters to your team members. Do they want time off to volunteer at their favorite charity or to attend a rally or demonstration to support a cause they are passionate about? That is where you can play a big role in supporting the purpose and meaning they care about in their lives.

Let's get a bit tactical around purpose. Why does it matter that the team updates the CRM system? It is part of their job, right? What is the purpose behind doing this? Your sellers are likely paid a base salary, and this is part of the work they are paid for as part of their base salary. It signals deal progress and pipeline status and feeds into your forecast. Your forecast signals to the company the revenue that can be expected from you and your team in a given quarter. This in turn unlocks investments and additional resources to support your ability to deliver that revenue. You are the link that provides the purpose as to why it matters for your sellers to do all of the administrative tasks they hate.

Why does forecast accuracy matter? Isn't it a virtue to under-forecast and overdeliver? Those late-quarter diving catches and heroic efforts are rewarded, right? Might want to rethink that. If you forecast 25 million but really think you can do 35 million, the lower, inaccurate number means you will receive less investment and resources to support your deals. The company does not have the confidence in your revenue outlook to support increased investment in hiring new sellers. You are doing yourself and your team a disservice by underforecasting. No sandbagging allowed. Forecasting a strong pipeline signals the strength of our business and that we're a good place to put more resources.

Your company's story of purpose can also provide thought leadership to your customers. This can give you an avenue to meet senior executives in new business functions that you normally would have difficulty accessing.

For example, Microsoft's cultural transformation has been widely written about in the press. It's a great story and customers are interested to learn how Microsoft transformed, the cultural initiatives Microsoft has in place, and the types of training provided to employees, many of which are also provided to customers. I've been on many calls with customer human resources executives who want to hear about our accessibility efforts and how we've built accessibility into our products, employee engagement initiatives, and the tools we use to support collaboration and engagement. These are a few examples of how a company's values and initiatives also create value for customers above and beyond what is sold.

Sustainability is another hot topic and Microsoft has carbon-neutral data centers and a pledge to be carbon neutral by 2030. Chief operating officers, CIOs, and the heads of real estate want to hear about these efforts and the metrics we use to track progress.

Maybe one of your seller's customers is a thought leader in a particular area of interest to your company. It strengthens the business relationship on both sides.

I've already shown data in Part I that employees want to work for a purpose-driven organization that aligns with their own values. It's a type of currency—flexibility and social mission can carry as much if not more weight than the hard currency of money. "Benefits" means more than just commission and stock options these days.

As the sales manager, it is your job to learn what your company is doing and stands for and use that to empower your sellers to have more compelling conversations with their customers to find areas of alignment and value exchange.

CHAPTER 21

Creating a
Love Your Team Culture

n the summer of 2021, I golfed with a gal who worked for me twenty years ago. Chris, my husband, who was also golfing with us, asked, "So what was it like working for Helen?"

Her answer was enlightening. I was smart, had content knowledge, and awareness of what the team was working on. I let her do her job and didn't micromanage, focusing instead on outcomes. I was available to them as needed. I addressed poor performance in other team members quickly and directly, thereby raising the bar for everybody by having high expectations. I helped facilitate a team dynamic that made her feel proud to be part of the team. For context, she worked remotely from where I was located as did a number of her peers.

Decades later, this former employee valued those traits in terms of managerial style. It's a style that may not be as common as others, but it is not unique, and it is all in service to creating a high-performing team with a culture that gets remembered for decades.

Much has been written about Microsoft's cultural shift under Satya Nadella when he took the helm in 2014. About eighteen months before the pandemic started, Microsoft rolled out a manager framework called Model, Coach, Care. Managers are expected to model the behavior they want to see in their team, coach the team, and care for them. There are courses available to managers to help them bring this to life. Satya credits this framework as being essential to Microsoft's success during this time while managers navigated the realities of the pandemic and the unique needs of each team member.

Empathy can be challenging to learn, especially for practical-minded managers focused on outcomes and the bottom line. Curiosity may be a more useful approach when thinking about conversational skills. Curiosity is all about seeking to understand, and it isn't rooted in emotion.

While all the skills outlined in the previous chapter can be employed in any conversation, it is also vital to think of the broader company culture and the skills and behaviors expected. Examples could be inclusion, always learning and growing, accountability, and allyship. A Love Your Team culture focuses on building trust, empathy, relationships, and high performance. These are foundational to effectively managing sales teams.

Sales managers have the most direct influence over their team's culture and how their team feels about their job and opportunity within the company. We set the tone as leaders. Our team members want to make sure their voice is heard and we understand them. Our goal is to create a healthy culture where team members feel free to be their best selves and do their best work.

A healthy, productive team culture promotes the following:

- High performance
- Individuals feel that they can be authentic
- Trying, failing, and learning from failures is okay
- Grace and understanding
- Trust-building
- Relationship-building/connection
- Suspension of judgment
- Seeking to understand first
- Open-mindedness, or some might say a growth mindset
- Empathy

Below I review the Love Your Team principles. I've added a few that were introduced in the conversation chapters. Finally, I outline how these principles can be applied to creating a Love Your Team culture.

REPRISE: LOVE YOUR TEAM PRINCIPLES

How we interact with our team matters. We want to create an opportunity for our team members to do their best work. To do that, they need to feel accepted, seen, understood, accommodated, respected, trusted, and valued.

This brings us back to the foundational principles of the Love Your Team system: trust, transparency, and caring. Authentic connection cannot happen without these principles, which are often established and reinforced in opportune micro-moments within conversations as other topics are discussed.

Trust

Establishing trust is essential for your team to feel safe and calm. It opens up the possibility that they will share with you what's going on in their lives that might affect their work and performance. If a team member "goes dark" and stops communicating with you and starts missing deadlines, find out what is going on. It might be a signal they are disengaged and searching for another job. It might also be that they are overwhelmed and need your help and perspective to see a path forward.

So, how do you build trust?

Chris Voss, a former hostage negotiator for the FBI, says the key to building trust is to show that you see the world through the other person's eyes. It's about acknowledging and showing the other person you know where they are coming from. Maybe a member of your team has too much work on their plate and cannot fulfill your expectations. Seeing the other's point of view and understanding where your team member is getting stuck is vital to moving forward.

Trust is a two-way street. Some team members will tell you everything the moment you introduce yourself. Some will be cautious about communicating much at all—either business or personal —until they get to know you better.

When I first took over as the manager of a twelve-person team there were two people who wanted a 1:1 scheduled every week. All others were happy with meeting every other week. I built stronger relationships more quickly with the two I met with weekly because of the increased frequency to connect. With each conversation, we built a better understanding of each other, the challenges facing them, and how I could help. Many of my team members, over time, would ping me on IM (instant message) when they needed a quick chat, irrespective of when our next 1:1 was scheduled. As a result, I would speak with some team members more than once a week even though our scheduled 1:1 was every other week. I endeavor to genuinely care and connect with my team during our scheduled 1:1s and in these small "How are you doing?" moments.

Another example from years ago is when one of my team members had a performance issue. I was new to him as a manager, and we did not have a trust-based relationship. I could see that the employee was reluctant to show that he did not have it all together. In short, he did not trust me to support him. I initiated a performance management process. By showing the team member that I did indeed care about his success and was willing to coach him and provide examples of what good performance looks like, I earned his trust. That team member ended up being one of my biggest fans and we are still in touch to this day.

Other team members are more guarded. Early in my tenure working with one team member, he and I would meet every other week. He talked about tactical work he was doing and upcoming executive meetings. He was focused on the day-to-day and delivered solid results. At some point, maybe three months into our working relationship, he asked about getting promoted, and I was not very supportive as I'd not seen the leadership required for him to move to the next level. He then asked for weekly 1:1 meetings with me so we had time to discuss more strategic initiatives he was working on with his customer and more nuanced discussion around his leadership of the extended team. This is a case where he was not inclined to share more than what was immediate and as a result, we both realized that my view of his performance was incomplete. As a result of this shift, I could see that he indeed was doing the work to warrant a promotion and that happened.

If discussing personal topics is uncomfortable at first, keep conversations business-oriented. For instance, a conversation could start like this: "You're doing an amazing job driving revenue, but I'm not seeing a lot of progress in building stronger executive relationships with your customers and this could limit our ability to grow our business. Can I be a resource to help you with those executive connections? Can we brainstorm strategies to build those connections?"

I always start conversations with my team members asking them how they are doing. Many of them start by talking about business topics. I've found that over time they will also start talking about personal circumstances, such as vacation or how they celebrate an upcoming holiday. Eventually, they will typically tell me about more personal areas of their life, such as challenges with kids or going through a divorce. Take your cue as to what they are ready to discuss. This is about supporting them, not being best buddies. I'm careful to not get too friendly with my team, meaning I want to keep it professional, and I don't spend time outside of work with one or two team members and not others.

Building trust with my team resembles building trust with customers. In fact, I think of my team as my number one customer. I've found that the most trust can be built when working through problems. When I listen to and address a customer complaint, that customer is more satisfied than ever. Even if I cannot fix their complaint, demonstrating empathy, listening, and taking the action within my control builds trust. The same goes for my team. Working through challenges with a team member deepens the relationship and creates more lasting trust. It does this more quickly than low-stakes interactions. I'm not advocating to instigate conflict, but if we embrace the conflict when it comes and do what we can to resolve it, we are building deeper trust and human connection.

This leads us directly to the next two Love Your Team principles, transparency and caring, which are essential for trust-building.

Transparency

Transparency filters through all other conversations, building trust along the way. It's a good-faith effort to be honest and open and helps mitigate misunderstandings and anxiety surrounding change. It contextualizes, gives details, explains reasons, and in general seeks to shine a light on any potential boogeymen hiding in the company or team shadows that might cause undue and unnecessary anxiety for the team and affect their work and well-being.

For example, in a 1:1 conversation, I'll say to a team member, "You know what? I'm feeling a little bit out of sorts because I'm not getting feedback or clarity myself, and I'm seeking that." This admission may at first look like weakness—after all, I've just admitted to being confused—but the employee invariably responds, "Oh, I thought it was just me."

Our admissions of not knowing or confusion allows the team members to voice their own confusions. And now we both can work toward clarity and understanding from a place of calm rather than frustration. I always circle back and share what I know that addresses the issue at hand, even if the answer is, "The issue is not yet ready to be shared broadly and I expect we will know more in sixty days." If you say you are going to do something, do it. This is essential for building and maintaining trust.

With my team, I offer my perspective on happenings within the company that matter to them. Even as we managers seek to satisfy our own curiosity, we need to acknowledge that our team is also curious. If this curiosity isn't assuaged by me or someone else in the leadership team, they will assuage it through grassroots channels, which may be less reliable.

It's okay to talk about what's going on within a company to reassure employees that inevitable change—change in business strategy, political winds, managers, and organization—does not mean disaster. A new company vice president may be less visible than the old one. It feels different to the team. Work goes remote for everyone. Team members are returning to the office. Team members need to talk it out to process changes, otherwise the unknowns often lead to worry.

While we seek to reassure, always maintain confidentiality and appropriateness about the inner workings of the company. For instance, it is not appropriate to disclose organizational changes in advance of the announcement. That creates havoc in the team and we risk our team members knowing pieces of information but not the whole plan or picture. Wait until there is a formal communication plan. It is likely that new changes leak out in some fashion. This creates the inevitable situation of some team members feeling left out while others seem to be in an inner privileged circle. The purpose of transparent conversations is to foster trust and not create feelings of favoritism and unfairness. I endeavor to treat everyone the same.

A caution here. We can promote transparency through modeling it, but don't demand it of your team. Admitting we don't know and revealing negative emotions is a vulnerable and humble position to be in, and employees have less power than us to begin with. We can invite transparency within personal conversations by asking, "Are you okay?" and making observations such as, "You seem stressed." But you must respect the employee's right to only share what they are comfortable sharing.

Caring

Caring for your team is just that, care. Give a damn. Be genuinely interested in how your team is doing and consider their needs before yours. Caring is not about their personal life; it spans all domains of work life too. You have skills, insights, relationships, and experience your team members need that when deployed will reduce sales friction, remove blockers, and enable them to exceed their revenue and other business goals. Your team is your number one customer. Employee expectations have changed as discussed in the Introduction. Caring for your team includes providing the flexibility they need while holding them accountable for delivering the results expected. Caring is supporting your team and helping them adapt to unforeseen or extenuating circumstances, and empathizing with the emotional demands of work and life.

Grace, or forgiving and adapting to unforeseen or extenuating circumstances, and empathizing with the emotional demands on team members living with these circumstances is all part of caring. It's all part of flexibility and treating workers like humans.

Empathy

A lot is said these days about the need for sales managers to be empathetic. Empathy is defined as really understanding what the other person is going through. Walking in their shoes is a metaphor. It is distinct from sympathy, which is feeling bad for the other person.

The Gartner Group says empathy is a critical skill for sales managers to be successful in a world where employees want managers to care about them more broadly as people, not as interchangeable parts. "Managers who display high levels of empathy have three times the impact on their employees' performance than those who display low levels of empathy," the Gartner Group says.[1] I sometimes mess up with customers and do not keep my commitments. I need empathy as well. Here's an example. My daughter gave birth to my first grandchild during the pandemic. I was only getting drops of information and tried to give my daughter and son-in-law space

---

[1] Brian Kropp, Alexia Cambon, and Sara Clark, "What Does It Mean to Be a Manager Today?" *Harvard Business Review*, April 15, 2021, https://hbr.org/2021/04/what-does-it-mean-to-be-a-manager-today.

while she labored. They went to the hospital at 2:30 a.m. I was tense and distracted the next day, wondering how she was doing. I missed a call I'd set up only an hour earlier with a customer. It was embarrassing. I completely forgot. Luckily the customer was understanding. I apologized, rescheduled, and we moved forward. This was a good reminder to be understanding and generous with my team when they miss deadlines or make a mistake. We all get distracted by big life moments involving those we care about. When my daughter called and I finally got to see her and the baby and knew things were okay, I felt much better. I was able to concentrate and focus on work again. I wasn't effective in keeping my calendar and calling this customer on top of that emotional demand.

These things happen. As sales managers, we can't control the circumstances, and we can't always prevent mistakes, but we can control how we respond to them. And these responses can either be helpful and supportive, or not. My experience and knowledge tell me that what is better for my team is better for achieving the results we are accountable for. A little understanding and forgiveness go a long way to maintaining a strong relationship with team members. It also leads to loyalty and renewed dedication.

ADDITIONAL PRINCIPLE: CURIOSITY

My own approach to conversations is one of curiosity. It's not only a principle but a learned skill used for framing questions and seeking to understand before passing judgment. It's a new (old) approach within the workplace. My own adoption of it occurred around 2016 when I learned it from a sales manager who worked for me. I noticed that she followed a principle that I thought of as "Seek to understand first. Don't jump to conclusions." I also noticed that she would pause rather than respond without thinking, an approach that is particularly helpful when emotions are aroused or triggered; take a breath and be curious. I recognized not only how I felt on the receiving end of that approach but also the strong connections she fostered with her team. She gained more clarity on situations and could then formulate a path forward that both she and her seller could agree to, one that made sense to both parties. I adopted her principle as my own to fully listen to what the other person is saying: I ask questions and try not to jump to conclusions. Sometimes this is easier said than done.

Being curious is one of the most relevant conversational skills you can adopt. It is also an overarching approach to life and work. To understand the situation at hand and not jump to conclusions based on what you assume, you must stop and be curious. Ask questions. How do you really know what the problem or issue is without probing? How can you craft an effective solution without knowing the problem you are trying to solve? So, another important principle a Love Your Team manager must take is one of curiosity.

Curiosity requires not being afraid of the truth. I'd rather be told the truth than be placated, especially if that truth affects my ability to support and manage my team. That's not always true of others, even as they espouse being open-minded. But true open-mindedness welcomes questions and criticism. It establishes you as someone who isn't afraid to tackle tough challenges. It can also build trust. Being curious and open-minded means you are willing to learn, grow, adapt, innovate, and change.

I use curiosity to clarify conversations. I seek to understand. I resist jumping to conclusions. I pause and try very hard not to react but rather get curious and ask questions. This is hard sometimes, especially when I'm emotionally triggered. I use open-ended questions and then get more specific. I use active listening skills and play back what I heard to ensure my understanding.

As you get into a conversation, part of the goal is to figure out what's going on and know when and how to pursue clarification of the context, intent, and content of the words the other person is saying. Curiosity helps refine understanding of the situation from all points of view and available data and evidence.

For example, I was having a conversation with a customer about a proposed MOU (memorandum of understanding) to govern the relationship and process over the course of a project. I was up front with my own bias, explaining that, in my experience, I hadn't seen these types of memorandums be effective, and I thought creating them wasn't worth the time. The customer explained the reason for an MOU again. After he laid out his case, I asked him if he had examples of these memorandums being effective and fulfilling the purpose intended. He thought about it and admitted he couldn't think of any examples. By being curious and asking questions, the customer agreed that it did make sense to move forward without an MOU.

Another example is internal. I often hear an executive say, "We want to invest in our customers." What does that mean? What kind of investment? Does that mean giving customers funds in the form of a discount? Or are we giving them skill-building trainings at no cost? Are we providing staff augmentation? What criteria is being applied to determine whether or not a customer qualifies for this incremental investment? Investing in customers could also mean we are investing our time and resources to learn more about our customers and be a student of them. How is this investment being measured? What purpose underlies the action? What outcomes are being sought?

Refinement of meaning occurs over time. Comprehension is a work in progress. As you iterate, you home in on the underlying need of the ask.

Here's another example: a seller asked for investment of resources to help with a sales pursuit. They were assigned a consultant to provide advice relevant to the sales pursuit. The seller actually wanted an extra pair of hands who would own the sales pursuit. When I circled back to check in on this team member's request, I got this clarification. As it turned out, there wasn't anybody available with the expertise to own the sales pursuit. So while there was a hiccup in comprehension and a mismatch of needs, at least the team member knew there was no option to provide them with the resource they desired.

Could I have employed more curiosity earlier to prevent the hiccup? Sure. We can always be better. But at least my continued curiosity as a manager helped mitigate further frustration, and even if the seller still didn't get the resource they wanted, at least they knew they were heard.

COMPANY CULTURE VS. TEAM CULTURE

It's easier to build a healthy, positive team culture when the company and surrounding organization you are a part of also has a healthy culture. While the company and larger organization you are a part of will have its own set of cultural expectations and norms, you have the opportunity to create your own internal microculture. You set the culture for your team.

What is culture? Culture is a set of behaviors, norms, standards, and ways of thinking that permeate an organization. You create the culture for your team. The team culture is set through your actions, what you say, how you treat others, how you care, and how you hold your team accountable for delivering results.

What kind of sales manager are you? What is your management style? What priorities do you focus on? Have you shared them with your team? Have you thought about the type of culture you want to build? My management approach is culture and people first, providing clear objectives and goals, coaching, empowering the team, being transparent, and building and leading a high-performing team. I share my priorities for the next ninety days so they know what I'm focused on. Another manager, a colleague of mine, has a management approach that encompasses inspiring, empowering, and appreciating her team.

Managers create a team culture every time they interact with and coach their team. Consistent approaches matter. Culture is built through all of the interactions you have over time. Culture is also created through how you hold your team members accountable for delivering results. Culture is created through how you uphold and practice the company's culture. Even in a company with a great culture, different teams will have their own flavor and extent to which they focus on and behave consistently with the company's culture.

Team cultures are shaped by your own values and expectations. These reside on top of the company expectations and values. Your team will pay more attention to your culture and values than the company's. If they don't like your approach, they will leave your team. You bring culture to life and your team members' experiences of their job is through you. The culture you create may complement your company's culture or may be counter to the company's culture. It is up to you.

This is where the Love Your Team principles reenter the picture. Trust, transparency, caring, empathy, and curiosity are necessary to be an effective sales manager. When these principles are aligned within your team through example, coaching, and accountability, they create an environment in which your team understands the behavioral expectations, there is open and honest communication, and team members care about and support each other. It creates greater team alignment, engagement, and satisfaction.

Since I've already discussed the principles that go into creating team culture, I focus here on the activities that apply these principles. These activities should look familiar, as many are done within the conversations explained throughout this book.

Activities that set the cultural tone:

Introduce your own values, priorities, leadership style, preferences, and goals in an introductory team meeting and initial 1:1 conversations.

Encourage the team to be open in every conversation.

Create a safe space for building trust by displaying your own trust and transparency.

Hold your team members accountable for delivering on performance expectations.

Address underperforming team members through a performance improvement plan leading to improvement of performance or loss of their job.

Creating a Love Your Team culture establishes a guiding purpose and set of values for your team. It gives them a North Star to follow when things get complicated and challenging, enabling them to make decisions on their own and ask for help without consequences.

As managers, we have the responsibility to create a culture within the sphere of our own team. That ability is informed by the company environment and culture. Sales managers have more power than they might think to create a microcosm of culture within an organization that does not have a healthy culture. Sometimes, I have found that the stress on me of creating a great team culture amid a poor culture is exhausting as I try to shield my team from the nonsense around us. We can only do as much as we can and there have been times when I've chosen to leave my role and take on a different management role inside another organization with a healthier culture.

As a sales manager, I rely on the resources provided by the company. These include training, career development, and mentoring resources, for example. As an example, if your company is not interested in supporting your team members in career development, it limits what you can offer and make available. There have been times when I've had a budget for training and discretion to hire outside trainers or approve team members taking a workshop outside the company. Every company has a different approach. Some companies provide training on how to live their stated cultural values such as inclusion, accessibility, flexibility, and collaboration training. The provided opportunities, values, and resources are important to team members. They influence whether a team member goes or stays.

Your best efforts as a manager to create a healthy team culture can help plug gaps in satisfaction left by a company's culture, but in the end it isn't sustainable. Think of teams that disperse all at once after a favored manager leaves. A sales manager needs to ask themselves if they can be successful building a team and asking for resources if they are limited in what they can offer. It's up to sales managers to choose whether or not to work in a culture where they can thrive.

There's only so much a sales manager can do if their team is not getting the value and values they want out of their job. There's deal-making here, too, and at the end of the day, teams vote with their feet, sales managers included. It is vital for retention and success that companies do their best to listen to and support their managers as much as the managers listen to and support their teams.

In the end, the best-loved team is one that's loved by the whole company, top to bottom.

Conclusion

Words matter. The "Sticks and Stones" playground rhyme is wrong. Words can hurt. And in terms of a business, they can create a culture of selfishness, distrust, dishonesty, retaliation, and dysfunction—a culture of quit. Great talent does not want to stick around a toxic culture, and critical to this discussion, they don't have to.

I am friends with a very capable seller who was recruited to join another team within her company. Once hired on, neither her manager nor her manager's manager who originally hired her reached out to see how she was doing, offer support, or engage with her in any way. She was told which accounts she was assigned and to "get to work." She left after a month, being recruited away by another company and another manager she had worked for in the past.

Sales managers may not always have control over a company's culture, but they do have control over the sales environment they create within that culture. This employee had been shocked to find that the company's stated values of team and individual support did not translate to the actual experience on the job.

Sales managers have an outsized impact on how a seller feels about their job and their decision to stay or go. With so many options available for top talent, quitting is easy. And when your top talent leaves, they often recruit their friends, the other sellers on your team.

I cannot overstate the importance of the sales manager for team engagement, satisfaction, and retention. It is the sales manager that establishes and maintains an environment of trust, support, and high performance. That is what matters to top talent.

Every company must be an innovation company or risk going out of business. It is your top sellers who generate the revenue from innovations that your company depends upon.

Sales managers are the linchpins that retain talent and provide a multiplier effect leading to outsized results. The revenue generation and growth machine only made possible by top sales talent and management is critical to our economy. This is an urgent issue. The innovation economy is here to stay, and if we are to be successful as a society, we have to be successful in selling the innovations that get created.

While all companies are becoming tech companies, it is the people who make and sell those innovations made possible by technology that are the difference makers.

Sales managers provide the support, resources, and coaching that enable sellers to do their best work. Those sellers, in turn, create trusting relationships with their customers who are betting their careers on the purchase decisions they are making. Sellers are the catalyst for monetizing innovations.

Traditionally, the value of sales management has been underrated, but companies are starting to realize the importance of this role. There is much talk in the press that 2022 will be the year of the sales manager. I'm skeptical. What does that mean? Where is the thought leadership and training to help sales managers understand what they need to do to be effective?

This is where the Love Your Team approach comes into play. It provides a framework and specific actionable conversations that all sales managers must have with their team. These conversations build trust, help sellers remove roadblocks, and ultimately deliver the value of innovations for their customers. The Love Your Team system outlines the conversations sales managers must also have with colleagues and internal stakeholders as well as with customers. It has been long overdue. The old way of selling and managing teams is no longer effective.

While there is a fantasy of calling sales a profession, in reality, there is no standardized approach that works. Unlike other professions, like accounting, engineering, and medicine, sales lack standards. There's no consistency, even at the highest executive levels. It's the Wild West. Companies cry out for more standardization, pining for a factory-like mode of production. It does not exist.

We've discussed a number of approaches and made the case that traditional sales management is no longer effective and a new approach is needed. Building strong team cultures, creating trust, and supporting your team's success will win out. That is how you retain top talent and build a high-performing team.

Everyone wants their managers and leaders to care about them, even if they don't feel confident saying so. They want managers to lend a helping hand and provide a greater level of resources and knowledge, even if they feel reluctant to ask for this help for fear of looking weak.

As managers, we can actively combat this false view of caring as weakness if we lead the way. We have the power to do this.

When you're a manager, domain expertise is only useful as far as it serves your team. There's nothing more important for a manager to do than get to know their team. You can't do anything as a manager—deliver results or revenue, build a high-performing team, grow pipeline, increase opportunities, or engage executives—if you don't know your team. This step comes even before getting to know customers or the ins and outs of the business. It's job number one.

People matter—as individuals with personal lives and drives that coexist with their work lives and ambitions, intertwined and sometimes overlapping.

Your team matters. If they can't work with their teammates toward a common goal, nothing gets done well.

Culture matters. Building a strong team culture where everyone feels valued, respected, and included matters. The company's culture matters too. As a sales manager, you can create your team culture and must do so.

You matter, as a generator of conversations, engaging and supporting your team and amplifying their success. Your company is depending on you to create a high-performing team that is able to sell your company's innovations and generate the revenue expected.

Be curious about your team. What do your team members care about? What are their ambitions? What do they want for support?

Be curious about yourself. Learn and grow. Which conversations will make the most impact on your team? Prioritize those and get good at having them. What could you do differently to build a better team culture? How will you become the manager that you would work for?

That's how to Love Your Team.

Acknowledgments

My children, Amara Bell and Derek Fanucci, who grew up in the midst of my career journey, which was not easy, especially when I was away from home and working at night.

Robin Fischer Blatt who so generously wrote a foreword and a testimonial and provided specific and well-thought-through suggestions immensely improving this book. Thank you!

The staff at Scribe Media, especially Barbara Boyd, my book coach, and Erin Mellor and KT Leota, my publishing managers, for keeping me on track and providing the guidance and confidence I needed to complete this project.

All of the people who have worked with me and for me over my career, especially since becoming a manager. I've learned so much from each of you. You've made me the manager and leader I am today.

A deep appreciation to John Hamm who has always been a sounding board for me when I needed it as well as a friend and mentor. Your words of wisdom echo in the pages of this book.

John Majeski, for your encouragement, support, and making my *Love Your Team* podcast required listening for the early-stage companies in your portfolio.

A special shout-out to Stacey Meston, Leslie Wood, David Charbonneau, Jeff Oberbillig, Ohad Richberg, Shivaprasad Mungara, Rahul Maniktala, Peggy Scott, Larry Chew, and Julie Lamphiear, who provided testimonials to be used in this book. Thank you for being willing to publicly endorse me, even though you had no idea exactly what this book was about. I appreciate your trust and confidence in me.

Finally, Chris Beall, my husband, who convinced me to have the audacity to write this book. This book definitely would never have happened without your support, patience, and the endless conversations about the content. Your foreword eloquently captures the relevance and value of this book for the reader. Thank you!

About the Author

ELEN FANUCCI is an MIT-trained engineer who has built her reputation and career managing teams responsible for billions of dollars of quota. She developed the Love Your Team system of sales management over a twenty-five-year career on the front lines at top tech companies including Apple, Sun Microsystems, IBM, and Microsoft. Helen hosts the *Love Your Team* podcast, which focuses on retaining top talent and building high-performing teams.

CPSIA information can be obtained
at www.ICGtesting.com
Printed in the USA
BVHW050344191022
649664BV00001B/4